presentation power

Presentation Power

Geoffrey X. Lane

Become a Powerful Speaker

Work Words
PUBLISHING

Requests for permission to reproduce any part of this book should be mailed to:
3rd Floor, 915 Fort Street
Victoria, B.C. V8V 3K3

Published by Work Words Publishing Inc.

Lane, Geoffrey, 1945-, author

Presentation power : become a powerful speaker / Geoffrey X. Lane.

Includes index.
Issued in print and electronic formats.
ISBN 978-0-9739648-2-0 (pbk.)
ISBN 978-0-9917854-0-7 (epub)

1. Public speaking. I. Title.

PN4129.15.L35 2013
808.5'1
C2013-906521-0

C2013-906522-9

Cover and interior artwork by Geoffrey X. Lane
Cover design by Geoffrey X. Lane and Jonathon Harris
Publishing strategy by Jesse Finkelstein and Trena White,
  Page Two Strategies
Interior design by Stacey Noyes, LuzForm Design
Editing by Shirarose Wilensky

I would like to acknowledge the gentle and loving support of Brigitte in writing this book.

CONTENTS

This book's guide to becoming a powerful speaker is organized around a simple but flexible analogy of archery. The elements are the archer, the bow and arrow, and the target. The four elements of archery represent the components of a great presentation experience.

The tools, research and strategies to turn anxiety into a source of energy. Learn how to focus and relax, tapping into the energy you need to become a powerful speaker. Tips and guidelines to increase your performance level and help you become an even more powerful speaker.

Chapter 3 **The Arrow**

Audience involvement and inspiration in storytelling. An overview of the creative process to help you develop and write a story, advice for writing the script for various kinds of presentations, story arc and presentation don'ts to keep you on track to becoming a powerful speaker.

Chapter 4 **The Bow** 87

Alternative strategies that engage the emotions to more effectively communicate with the audience. A selection of the available presentation tools and resources at your disposal and a handy presentation checklist.

Chapter 5 **The Target** 113

You, the speaker, and how you interact with the audience. The audience and what you need to know about them to be a powerful speaker.

Conclusion **You Have a Choice** 133

The Million Dollar Coach

Recently, I was introduced as the "Million Dollar Coach." I was surprised by this title, as I had never thought of myself that way. Afterwards, I asked why that introduction was used and was told simply "well, it is true; that's why we hire you." Yes, it is true that in 2012–13, I have helped teams win more than $300 million in contracts. What a great year, and what fun it was, too.

When people ask what I do, I respond by saying "I am a presentation director." What is that? you may ask.

Well, I made up that name to explain what I do as a consultant coach for presentation teams. I direct and coach teams and individuals to present their ideas with authenticity, drawing out their personal power and charisma, and as a result, they get more of what they want, with more ease and with a sense of fun. As the Oscar-winning director Robert Altman once said, "The role of the director is to create a space where they can become more than they've ever been before, more than they've dreamed of being." It might sound simple, but it is challenging, exciting, sometimes stressful and occasionally disappointing.

I love winning—what I really mean is that I love helping people to win business, win the interview, win the job. It is so satisfying to see the people, teams and organizations that I have coached do well. Oh, yes, I am competitive, and when we win—elation!

This is how my career as presentation director started. It all began when I was asked to coach and prepare a nervous but eager and very bright Andrea Shaw for a special interview. We spent the next three days in front of a video camera. At first it was difficult for Andrea, but with coaching, presenting and more coaching, she became a very good speaker. Only later did I find out that she won the position as media liaison for the Vancouver Winter Olympic bid team. Sometime later, Andrea introduced me to John Furlong, the president/CEO, and Jack Poole, the chair, of the 2010 Winter Olympic bid team.

Six months had passed when I got a call from a man called Terry Wright asking me to help the 2010 Winter Olympic bid team prepare for the upcoming visit by the International Olympic Committee. This was a critical step in the evaluation process in winning the right to host the Olympics. When I arrived, Jack Poole asked me why I had decided to work for them. My answer was simple: "I want my young granddaughter Alexandra to see an Olympic event in her hometown."

I then worked for three weeks, prepping the individual speakers and teams that were to present to the IOC. The pressure was enormous—all of Canada was watching. It was an exciting and arduous task. Many of the team members were toppling from the pressure. Often, they wanted to convey copious amounts of technical information, an avalanche of data, yet the IOC had been very specific about the time allowed for the presentation and what direct questions needed to be answered. Getting the message down to three minutes was tough and required sharp editing.

The IOC visit was three intense days of presenting, meeting and socializing, we were continually judged, prodded and asked questions. Finally, it was over, all was quiet, but the questions were now replaced by worries about how we did and whether we had done enough. The IOC interviewed six other cities; it was nail-biting time. It took almost three months before we received the news that we had made it through to the next round! I felt part of me relax. We had made it this far.

Then I got a call about prepping the team for the critical final presentation before the full International Olympic Committee in Prague—this time, the whole world would be watching! I was excited, feeling the pressure and wanting to win for Canada. I met with John Furlong and Jack Poole to talk about the upcoming presentation in Prague, and as I was giving them some insights, they asked me what flight I was on. When I replied that I didn't have a ticket, there was a strained silence. John immediately picked up the phone, and I was now on the list. I went home to pack and left that very night, feeling excited and scared at the same time.

I arrived in Prague to find the logistics team well prepared, since they had already trained with me for the first presentation round. I met with most of the presenting team and then coached Premier Gordon Campbell; Olympians Catriona LeMay Doan, Charmaine Crooks and Steve Podborski; bid chairman Jack Poole; and the amazing John Furlong. Several people were arriving later, including Prime Minister Jean Chrétien and Wayne Gretzky, and I coached those who requested it. It was five days of intensive, pressure-packed rehearsals, rewrites and personal adjustments.

The presenters' experience levels and speaking styles were all over the place, from polished politician to overawed amateur. It was like herding cats, eight distinctly different cats all wanting to do their individual best for the team. And, yes, I did get scratched a couple of times—nothing serious; a good Scotch healed most of them. Many of the presenters had experience in and ideas about presenting; some needed and wanted coaching. The athletes were the easiest to coach, mostly because they were used to coaches and they wanted to win. The challenge was to build a presentation using all of these diverse speakers/athletes/politicians so that it looked, felt and was experienced as a team.

We developed a theme: why Canada's values were like the values of the Olympic ideal. I encouraged each presenter to speak about the theme as a personal story. This acted as the connector between the individual presenters and became the story for the presentation—a strongly woven chain supported by great audiovisuals.

After several full-tilt eighteen-hour-plus days, it was time to deliver. The team was amazing, following the script and cues I had written for them while looking effortless and polished onscreen. Three solid days of rehearsals and years of preparation paid off. We won the right to host the 2010 Winter Olympics. The 2010 Winter Olympics in Vancouver and Whistler, B.C., were a huge success, and the credit goes to the amazing team John Furlong put together. And, yes, my granddaughter got to see an Olympic event in her hometown.

Using the practical insights and knowledge gained from my experience as a speaker, trainer and facilitator, and from the intense pressure cooker of preparing for the Olympic bid, I have written this book. This book can mark the beginning of your path to becoming a persuasive and powerful speaker. There is no short cut; however, this book will help make it easier, much easier. The journey will take hard work and focus, and practical experience will further enhance and strengthen your abilities as a communicator and presenter. As a presentation director and consultant for many companies, organizations and individuals, I have helped raise and win more than $550 million in contracts and investment funds. The practical insights that have helped others I now offer you here.

Geoffrey Lane

CHAPTER 1

The Archer Model

The Archer   The Bow & Arrow   The Target

I magine standing on an old English green. The spring sunlight throws shadows on the ground. You have a bow in your hand and three arrows stuck point first in the ground beside you. It is your turn to shoot. You look down the green and at the end is a target covered in a cloth with a bull's eye painted on it. The crowd noise drops to a quiet murmur; there is a slight breeze upon your face. You pick up an arrow and, notching it on the bowstring, draw it back, focusing intently, holding the string, not letting the arrow fly until you are ready. Whoosh! It leaves your fingers, flying towards the target. Thwack! It penetrates the target. A spontaneous round of applause and cheers breaks the tense silence when you hit the bull's eye.

This book's guide to becoming a powerful speaker is organized around a simple but flexible analogy of archery. The elements are the archer, the bow and arrow, and the target. The four elements of archery represent the components of a great presentation experience:

- *the archer represents you, the speaker;*
- *the arrow is your story, your message;*
- *the bow represents the tools you use to deliver your presentation;*
- *and the target is your audience.*

The Archer

(you, the speaker) provides the power, energy, focus and vision to shoot the arrow to the target. Learning how to manage, maintain and develop that energy is important and forms a major part of any presentation. The mind of the archer focuses clearly on the target, determining purpose, expected outcome, timing and speed. The speaker's focus gives direction to the presentation so that the arrow can hit the target. The ground that the archer stands upon represents your knowledge of the subject matter to be presented and your skill at presenting. Your power as the archer comes from your passion and your authenticity.

The Arrow

represents your story to be told. All presentations must tell a story—just like a movie, TV show or advertisement. It is the structure and storyline that matter, whether the presentation is sixty minutes, six minutes or sixty seconds long. Without structure and story, your presentation will have little or no impact. I have seen energetic presenters give it their all, only to discover that no one remembered what they said! Using the power of story to involve and inspire the audience is essential to success in getting your ideas across.

The Bow

represents the media through which you deliver your story, such as slides, handouts, a flip chart, an iPad or direct access to the web. Just as the bow supplies energy to the flight of the arrow, your tools support and enhance your story or, if poorly chosen, block or diminish it. It is critical to choose the most effective media, based on the audience, the venue and the story to be told.

The Target

represents the audience. Audience members preselect the type of event they wish to attend, whether for business, education or some other purpose based on self-interest. As a presenter, you need to know what that self-interest is; this is what motivates, interests and affects your audience. If it is announced that you are speaking about yoga but then start speaking about financial planning, you have ignored what motivated the audience to attend your presentation.

Each of the four elements of the archer model is a study by itself, which I will discuss individually in the following chapters.

CHAPTER 2

☾ The Archer

"To conquer fear is the beginning of wisdom."
— Bertrand Russell

The focus of this chapter is you, the presenter, and to provide insights and tools to help you develop the energy required to make you a better presenter. You supply the energy needed to shoot the arrow to the target. It is imperative to learn how to manage, maintain and develop that energy to create a powerful presentation.

This chapter is divided into two sections:

The first section shares the tools, research and strategies to turn anxiety into a source of energy. Learn how to focus and relax, tapping into the energy you need to become a powerful speaker.

And the second section explains tips and guidelines to increase your performance level and help you become an even more powerful speaker.

Turn Your Fear Into Power

Focus and Results

What you focus on, you create more of.

I know this is a simple statement, but it is true. If before and during a presentation your focus is on your fears, you will experience them. Here is a simple rule that works:

The more I focus on myself and my fears, the more anxiety I experience.

The more I focus on my audience and their needs, the less anxiety I experience.

Change Your Mind

We all have injunctions, stopping phrases and old beliefs that prevent us from doing our best. If you can change your mind, you just might escape your limiting beliefs about— well, almost anything.

If you think you can, I know you will.
If you think you can't, I know you won't.
Speak publicly that is.

The Number One Fear in North America

According to *The Book of Lists*, the fear of public speaking ranks number one in the minds of the majority of people. This statistic has been repeated so often that it has become accepted "fact." This is NOT fact; it's a list collected from randomly selected people (in fact, the sampling was very small and it was not a scientific study)! It serves those who sell workshops and books on public speaking. Do some people genuinely have a phobia? Yes, but they are NOT the majority of people. Does this mean you have to fear public speaking? NO.

I believe it is unhealthy to believe in myths. How do I know the prevalence of the fear of public speaking is a myth? I have seen thousands overcome it in a few minutes; the Presentation Power workshop graduates are living proof. Nothing can prevent you from becoming a powerful speaker, other than accepting these social myths or old belief patterns. The old myth that public speaking is scary and very hard to do is a limiting belief that precludes possibility thinking. Anyone can learn to speak publicly and do very well at it! It is teachable and learnable.

Handling Fear & Anxiety

Do you see the world as it is or as you are? A key part of confidence is having a clear picture of yourself as you are now, to be in what I call "current reality." When I coached leaders who are having confidence or anxiety problems, it was often their self-perception that was out of whack. They were hanging on to an incident from the past and the fear that it was going to happen again—right now! Both will hinder or, in some extreme circumstances, cripple an otherwise powerful person.

I was not in current reality when I first got up to speak, as I experienced what is called in the theater a "flop sweat." While I waited backstage, I started to sweat—not perspire but sweat as if I was working out. I also ran to the bathroom and threw up. Fortunately, my dark jacket covered up the sweat stains. I also froze onstage and couldn't talk. If I had been in current reality, I would have said to myself, "Geoffrey, you are an accomplished professional, with ideas and tech-niques that work, and this is a conversation with peers. Just tell them the story of how and why your method works. Re-lax and have some fun." But at the time, the sponsor had to save me by quickly interviewing me. After, he asked me what that was about; truthfully, I did not know. It was about my unconscious and unchallenged assumption that what had occurred in the past was certain to repeat itself.

Later, when the shakes and heart pounding had subsided, I remembered an incident from high school. It was a sunny afternoon, girls were playing field hockey outside and I was watching them through the window, daydreaming as only a thirteen-year-old boy can. Suddenly, the teacher asked me a question: "What did Romeo say next?" Of course I did not know, as I had not been paying attention. I was then invited, more like ordered, to the front of the room.

Shakespeare book in hand, I went forward. I was to read Romeo's speech to Juliet while she is on the balcony. I have dyslexia and stress makes the words almost unintelligible, and to make things worse, the teacher asked the prettiest girl in the class, whom I had a crush on, to be Juliet. I made a terrible fool of myself and mispronounced words—it was as though my mind had gotten a terrible scrambling virus from brain to tongue. To me, it was the end of the world; I was shamed before my peers, laughed at in the corridor. As you can imagine, my nickname in that class was Romeo.

Because the human mind (particularly under stress) has difficulty knowing the difference between a real and imag-ined experience, here I was, twenty-seven when I made my first paid speech, but my emotional memory was triggered by that old classroom experience and I felt like that thirteen-year-old again, with all of the fears of embarrassment and social impact. The trauma of that humiliation created an emotional block about public speaking—until I challenged it!

The Greatest Myth

There is no such thing as a natural born speaker. It's a myth of epic proportions—we cannot even talk when we are born! I get very energetic on this topic. Many people believe they can just power through a performance, using energy and volume. Nothing could be further from the truth. I am sure you've heard the phrase "they were an overnight success," but the rest of the story is that most "overnight" successes worked hard at their craft long before they became successful.

Something clicked for me when I read *Talent Is Overrated* by Geoff Colvin. The book confirmed what I already knew: the very best professional speakers have worked, studied, been coached and made a major investment in their craft. According to Colvin, talent is overrated, and "the best performers have set highly specific, technique-based goals and strategies for themselves; they have thought through exactly how they intend to achieve what they want."

Beliefs & Myths

Because beliefs influence what we think and how we feel, it is important to look at why the myth of needing to fear public speaking persists today. If you grow up in a family or culture that believes this myth, you will too, until you challenge it. If your family and cultural background encouraged and rewarded self-expression, you will not have this fear or anxiety. Our past experience, cultural background, education and experience help us determine our truth about the world. Our beliefs determine our feelings, initiate our actions, motivate our reactions and create our results. If your truth is "I fear public speaking," then when you get up to speak, you will expect to experience symptoms of anxiety, which leads to feeling even more stressed, which leads to poor performance, which leads to poor results, which in turn supports your belief. You can then say "I was right!"

Rarely do we ask the tough questions about generally accepted beliefs. Today, we laugh at the idea that the world is flat and that if you sailed to the edge you would fall into the abyss. This was an accepted belief for several centuries, preventing exploration and creating fear in all sailors. New knowledge, current research and enquiring minds are continually upsetting old knowledge and the myths that resulted from lack of knowledge.

If you believe that you can, you will.

If you have a false negative belief about public speaking, you can inadvertently set up a self-reinforcing cycle of anxiety and failure:

Because I think what I think (fear of public speaking), I feel what I feel (anxiety)...

Because I feel what I feel (anxiety), I do what I do (shake, forget my speech and mumble)...

Because I do what I do (shake, forget my speech), I get what I get (a poor review and criticism)...

Which reinforces what I believe: I should and must fear public speaking. This is self-reinforcing false thinking:

if I think I can't, I won't.

The Myth Model

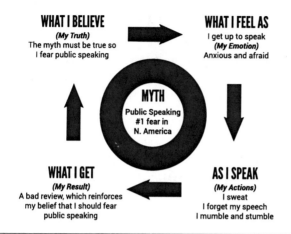

WHAT I BELIEVE
(My Truth)
The myth must be true so
I fear public speaking

WHAT I FEEL AS
I get up to speak
(My Emotion)
Anxious and afraid

MYTH
Public Speaking
#1 fear in
N. America

WHAT I GET
(My Result)
A bad review, which reinforces
my belief that I should fear
public speaking

AS I SPEAK
(My Actions)
I sweat
I forget my speech
I mumble and stumble

People tend to perceive events in terms of their emotional experience (I had a terrifying time public speaking). They also read what they want to see into events (It was terrifying speaking in public). Emotional anchors are very powerful inhibitors and can put blinders on the finest mind. People are inclined to select, interpret and filter external stimuli through their previous experiences, cultural values and acquired convictions. For the same reason, they tend to reject everything that does not fit.

As a result, it is often necessary to be aware of any interpretation of reality that is too rigid or is based on faulty perceptions. It is a challenge for most people to learn how to be aware of their perceptions and judgments, while maintaining vigilant awareness of their own biases. It is just so comfortable to hold on to what we "know" to be true. It is easy to believe that my point of view is the real "truth"; however, everyone has a different point of view, a different "truth," and that is the origin of the challenge and difficulty of human communication.

It is my experience that most of us are fairly good at dealing with the day to day, but we don't regularly bring our internal résumé up to date and we forget what we have accomplished and achieved. The past is no indication of future results—good or bad. What you focus on, you create, with or without your awareness. I now believe that it is fun and exciting to get up to speak. What do you believe?

The Reptilian Brain & the Fight-or-Flight Response

So what goes on in your brain and body when you get up to speak? It helps to understand that many of the sensations you experience in your body have their origins in the survival mechanisms of the human species; in other words, "it's all natural." It is easy to interpret the physical sensations you experience as "fear," but new knowledge now indicates this is the ancient (reptilian) brain trying to protect you from perceived danger. "We move away from pain; we move towards pleasure" is the reptilian brain's program for survival of the species.

The Fight-or-Flight Response
The Unconscious Motivation: Survival
The Prime Directive: Keep you safe
The Flight/Fight Response

we move away from pain   **we move towards pleasure**

When you're in real or perceived danger, your reptilian brain responds to the sense of threat and prepares you to survive. When you're presenting in public, your reptilian brain stimulates the adrenal glands, because of perceived danger. You then experience a cascade of hormones that causes our body to undergo a series of very dramatic changes that comprise the stress response, also known as the fight-or-flight response.

By its very nature, the fight-or-flight response bypasses our rational mind and moves us into "attack-or-run" mode. We may overreact to the slightest comment. Our fear is exaggerated. Our thinking is distorted. We see everything through the filter of possible danger. We narrow our focus to those things that can harm us. Fear becomes the lens through which we see the immediate world. We lose contact with our brain's frontal lobes, where logical or rational thinking reside. Our respiratory rate increases and blood is shunted to our muscles and limbs, which require extra energy and fuel for running and fighting. Our pupils dilate. Our awareness intensifies. Our sight sharpens. Our impulses quicken. Our perception of pain diminishes. Our immune system mobilizes with increased activation. We become prepared—physically and psychologically—for fight or flight.

Adrenaline is the most well-known hormone released during the fight-or-flight response, though each of the hormones, including noradrenaline, cortisol, and various other catecholamines and corticosteroids, plays a part. The effects include hyperarousal, increased blood flow, heightened pulse rate and increased physical performance, which the experienced speaker considers an enjoyable and invigorating state of mind and body but the inexperienced speaker perceives as "nerves" or "stress." These are normal and perfectly natural responses to getting up to speak. If you want to become a powerful speaker, it helps to have some awareness of how these natural chemical reactions of the brain work so that you are in your best state when presenting.

Adrenaline

Adrenaline is one of the many natural chemicals that course through your body when you are speaking publicly. The positive effect is to enhance your ability to read your audience and to think on your feet. All performers learn how to harness adrenaline to create a powerful impact. Presenters, trainers and facilitators learn that adrenaline has to be managed if they are going to deliver a well-paced presentation and not burn out.

We all have a limited amount of adrenaline in our bodies—say about three hours' worth a day. If you skip breakfast, drive fast to the event and then have five cups of coffee before 11 a.m., you can quickly use up this limited supply and then spend the rest of the day running on empty. If you then have to deliver a high-energy session at 3 p.m., you won't be in your peak state.

Unlike a car that stops when it runs out of gas, the human body has several emergency systems to kick in and keep you going when you are running on empty. This gives us the ability to survive when we're in real danger. Problems occur when people live in a constant state of perceived or real emergency, perpetually using their emergency system to keep going. Adrenaline abuse (or even addiction to stress situations) increases cholesterol, and excessive cortisol (a result of running on empty) leads to anxiety.

When you have used up your day's supply of adrenaline, your body will use cortisol to keep going. This is the drug of anxiety and fear. If you find yourself feeling shaky and anxious the day after a speaking event or training day, you have used up your adrenal supply and probably used cortisol to keep going.

It is also possible to burn out your adrenal system completely. Although adrenal burnout is a rare occurrence, I have never forgotten when it happened to me. I burnt out my adrenal system after twenty-four days on the road speaking in four different cities, three five-day workshops back to back and two speaking gigs. Then I crashed, spent three days in hospital and had to take a month off to recuperate. Be warned: you will feel elated and excited as you become a powerful speaker and might be tempted to overdo it. There's a price to pay. When you read that a superstar performer is in the hospital or behaving rather weirdly, it is more likely because of adrenaline burnout than drug abuse. This is actually exhaustion.

Serotonin

I have left the stage after delivering one of my best sessions or speeches and had that hollow feeling in my gut. I now know I was experiencing a serotonin low because I gave it my all (adrenaline) onstage. Serotonin and adrenaline are linked; use up one and the other also disappears. This is when I feel "wired but tired" and can't get to sleep, similar to jet lag. Often, the loneliness of traveling, or of being the leader and speaking, is less about loneliness and more about living an adrenaline-driven life and not knowing how to balance the corresponding decrease in serotonin. If your adrenaline and serotonin are out of balance, it becomes very hard to be what you are trying to inspire others to be. Learning to refresh and relax before and after a presentation is essential to long-term success.

Ways to Turn Your Anxiety into Energy

Visualization and Relaxation

One amazing gift of coaching the speakers for the 2010 Winter Olympic bid was working with the Olympic athletes. First, they were used to being coached and as such did not resist coaching, and second, they understood the power of visualization. As athletes, they practice seeing themselves doing a movement and doing it well, not just once but many, many times, until it is imprinted in their mind. They train their minds to help them succeed; remember, what you focus on, you create!

Take some time to do this exercise: Find a quiet space where you will not be disturbed and lie down if possible. Make yourself comfortable, take three slow breaths and begin.

Visualize yourself getting ready to give your presentation, getting dressed. What are you wearing as you go to the front of the room? Now see yourself at the front of the room, giving your presentation. Notice how relaxed and comfortable you look. Now see the audience, nodding in agreement, smiling as you speak. Notice how good you look and how happy the audience is. Hear the applause as you finish. Well done.

Deep Breathing

To minimize the effects of stress and prevent activation of the fight-or-flight response, it is important to practice patterns that lead to de-escalation. In that highly stressed state, that condition in which your brain is flooded with electrochemicals, you still have options. You do not need to be stressed—you can choose a different state. After all, these chemicals do not persist; they will dissipate in three to six seconds, with some help.

Deep breathing relieves stress and anxiety because of its physiological effect on the nervous system. Breathing slowly and mindfully activates the hypothalamus, which is connected to the pituitary gland in the brain, to send out neurohormones that inhibit stress-producing hormones and trigger a relaxation response in the body. The hypothalamus links the nervous system to the endocrine system, which secretes the hormones that regulate all activities throughout the body.

The following technique consists of taking three slow, deep breaths to slow things down. Count silently and slowly to six as you breathe in through your nose, and push your stomach out rather than your chest. This allows you to breathe with your diaphragm and to get a deeper breath. Then breathe out through your mouth on a slow count of six. As you breathe out, say the word "relax." Be sure to pace your exhale so that you have some breath left by the time you get to six. If you feel light-headed, slow it down a bit. Repeat three times.

Practice this technique each time you are aware of stress and eventually it will kick in automatically when you have a stressful situation. This simple technique can slow and even stop the fight-or-flight response.

Food & Drink

On the day of your presentation, or the day before if you are speaking first thing in the morning, eat what you know is good for you. Avoid eating or drinking anything you haven't had before, and beware of spicy and rich foods, as your system is already under some stress. Relax and stick with your favorite foods and drinks. Don't eat too much or too little. The process of digestion requires a great deal of energy, and a large meal will use up the energy you need for your presentation.

Avoid diuretics, notably caffeine drinks (coffee, tea and soft drinks). Drink water to hydrate before and during your speech. Avoid alcohol entirely before speaking, and don't take drugs or smoke marijuana. I hope it is common sense not to get intoxicated. Even a small amount can impair your cognitive abilities, and you need to be at peak efficiency. Don't listen to anyone who encourages you "to calm your nerves." It may calm your nerves, but it will also have a negative effect on your judgment—and that's always a bad thing with a microphone in your hand and an audience with smartphones.

The Day Before the Presentation

Before the day of the presentation arrives, make sure you do all of the little things that help your body and mind control anxiety. Get a good night's sleep the night before so that you're fully rested. Ensure you're properly hydrated and that you've had small and healthy meals. Go jogging or do another physical activity to relieve some of your muscle tension.

Prepare everything you need in advance so that you don't have any worries about being ready. Use the visualization techniques again, or integrate relaxation strategies, such as:

Progressive muscle relaxation
Make love not war
Get a massage
Meditation
Exercise
Yoga

The less anxiety you experience the day before, the better your performance will be. Anticipation can be one of the best parts of the journey. Anticipate doing well and build up a positive focus; it will decrease the negative effects of stress. What you focus on, you create.

Power & Performance

Motivation

"What's my motivation?" is a question actors ask to help them get into character; without motivation, they have no sense of what drives someone to do what they do and to act how they act. "What's my motivation?" is also a question that everyone asks themselves subconsciously, some consciously, every day, all the time. In fact, it's the first question you may have asked yourself when you were deciding whether to buy this book.

What kind of speaker do you want to become? The answer to that question determines your effort and commitment. If your vision is ambiguous, you will have no definite goal or time frame. A cloudy, unfinished vision won't properly motivate you, and you will probably fail. Or you will just avoid presenting altogether, even if you purchased this book. Develop a clear vision of the kind of speaker you want to become and then set a date to start.

What is your purpose as a speaker? Is it to get applause or to share your knowledge, skill and wisdom? If it is to get applause for your performance, perhaps becoming an actor would be more rewarding. Yes, you are expected to perform—all presentations are performances. However, they are radically different from acting. The actor has a script, stage direction and a director; the presenter has only himself—yep, that's it, just you. As a speaker, you are the scriptwriter, producer, director and performer. Unless you are the head of a major corporation or running for political office, in which case you will have the resources of a professional speechwriter and presentation coach. Is that fair? No. But if you have some fun and let go of any need to be "perfect," I know you will succeed.

The Perfection Trap

Perfectionists, like high achievers, tend to set high goals and work hard to attain them. However, a high achiever can be satisfied with doing a great job and reaching excellence (or something close), even if they don't completely meet their very high goals. Whereas perfectionists will accept nothing less than, well, perfection. "Almost perfect" is seen as failure.

What is the "perfection trap"? Often, by working so hard to be perfect, the speaker destroys their own authenticity— their ability to show up. Audiences love to hear real people talking to them; they recognize a polished performance but consistently want real people. Power as a speaker comes from you, from your authenticity. When it is "you" speaking, not you playing a role or "acting," the audience gets you. Everyone has what I call a built-in "BS meter," and we all know when someone is BSing their way through. Never "fake it till you make it." The only person you will fake out is you; the rest of us will have our BS meters buzzing loudly.

Although an audience will recognize a perfect performance, they will not relate to or buy from the perfect speaker or presentation—they're just too intimidating and demanding. A perfect presenter or presentation also reminds them of their imperfections. The audience won't and doesn't care about your drive to be perfect. They expect you to perform and want you to have some fun while you're doing it. My

greatest teachers about communication have been three-
and four-year-old kids, because they aren't bound by pre-
conceived ideas or social rules. So they are always just themselves. As we get older and gain responsibilities, we start to
change our natural authentic expression, inhibiting our
ability to communicate. Be yourself. Now that is something
that you can do better than anyone else. Listen to your inner
voice, relax and go for it.

Authenticity

Authenticity is your source of energy and power and audiences can spot a speaker who is "acting" rather quickly,
as authenticity is missing from the presentation. Often,
the novice speaker will try to be just like a speaker they admire, copying gestures, dress style, voice and speech patterns. This is how children learn, by first copying the adults
around them. I suggest you write down the traits and skills
of the speakers you admire the most. Then ask yourself a
question: "Do I have those?" This is not to discourage you
but to encourage you to keep your authenticity intact. The
more you copy, the easier it is to lose yourself. Be inspired by
the speakers you admire, learn what makes them such great
speakers, but put your own spin on it.

Should I try to be charismatic or just be me? I don't think
they are mutually exclusive! The most authentic speakers
are also the most charismatic. Often, authenticity is dis-
missed, yet this means that we are ignoring the effect it has
upon people and the world. It's tough to be authentic and
charismatic if your interactions don't have passion, humor
or some other element of emotion and human connection.
Show up and be real. If you're too buttoned-up and reserved,
it's hard to truly connect with people. Think about when
you're at home with your children or out with friends and

remember that feeling, tapping into it when you're making a presentation and want to motivate the audience.

I believe every human has four endowments: self-awareness, conscience, independent will and creative imagination. These give us the ultimate human freedom: the power to choose, to respond, to change and to act. Self-awareness informs and defines us, and conscience creates boundaries of behavior. Independent will provides us with the opportunity to learn and grow. Creative imagination allows us to see what otherwise would be in darkness. These endowments form and inform our authenticity.

Your authenticity becomes, in effect, your brand. As Warren Bennis and Joan Goldsmith wrote in their book, *Learning to Lead,* "to be authentic is literally to be your own author (the words derive from the same Greek root), to discover your native energies and desires, and then find your own way of acting on them." Your authenticity separates and differentiates you from everyone else on the planet. I love people who are authentic and show up. I love authentic brands. And I believe the opportunity for you to become a powerful speaker is available to you. To me, it is simple: a combination of clarity, creativity, authenticity and meaning. The result: a speaker that makes an emotional connection and uses symbolism, stories and all five senses. That speaker is remarkable. Not because of style or performance, but because they are authentic.

Show Up

I admire people when they "show up" and express themselves authentically. There is much fear in our world, and fear is often the reason we hide or reveal only what we consider to be acceptable about ourselves. I believe that the fear of revealing who we are is greatly misunderstood and that that fear somehow equals rejection by others. Yet most of us know instinctively when someone is hiding (i.e., not showing up or BSing), and consequently we do not trust them enough to reveal ourselves to them or to accept them for who they appear to be. When you speak authentically, you are giving the audience the natural you. You are keeping your own promise to show up in the world. In the words of Joseph Campbell, "We must be willing to get rid of the life we've planned, so as to have the life that is waiting for us. The old skin has to be shed before the new one can come."

Being authentic is one of the greatest gifts we can offer other human beings and ourselves. Our relationships improve and we experience less stress as a direct result of not hiding who we are. We develop deeper and longer-lasting friendships. Others in our community tend to trust us. The experience of the world seems more real. Those who, by age or wisdom, live in the state of authenticity are revered, respected, loved and admired.

In today's business world, we are increasingly being called upon to show up or, if you prefer, be authentic. Because we now communicate so much by e-mail, voice mail, fax, and the Internet, the need for interpersonal communication is continually growing. The more we use technology to communicate with each other, the greater our need for face-to-face communication and the more we crave the authenticity of personal contact. Nothing replaces the nuances of tone and pitch of a human voice or the facial and physical expressions of you, the communicator. But because we are using these skills less and less, we are losing our ability to show up. Words are only part of the messages we send to each other; the emotion and intent are carried and amplified by the body language and sound of the human voice.

When I show up (being myself), the audience hears me

in a very different way, a way that starts to build the relationship and deepen the understanding between listener and speaker. This creates an opportunity for a genuine exchange to take place. Communicating in person is the most powerful form of human interaction. To be truly successful, my advice is: always show up.

Enthusiasm & Passion

A powerful speaker is driven by passion and the desire to share knowledge and experience with others, to help others. One of the ways in which we show up for a presentation is with our enthusiasm. This is often suppressed by the novice speaker, as they wish to appear professional or cool and not overly excited. The audience requires that you show up and be real, not slick and polished. Here is an idea: if you cannot muster at least a small amount of real conviction for the subject of your talk, perhaps someone else should give it. If you appear not to care, neither will the audience. All energy is contagious, but particularly enthusiasm. Let your audience know that you are committed to your ideas and that you are excited about them. They will not only see your enthusiasm; they will feel it and get a glimpse of your authenticity. It is impossible to believe in something and not show it. Remember, we judge others by their behavior; we judge ourselves by our intentions. Give yourself permission to release your passion so that your audience knows how you feel. If you try to plow through a presentation, the audience will react to you, rather than listen to or be inspired by you.

Energy and enthusiasm are not exclusive to a coach's pep talk. There are many ways to express your enthusiasm. Think of a time when you were full of that energy and remember what it felt like. Use that memory of past enthusiasm to connect with today, then let it flow. You may speak softly with heartfelt enthusiasm. You may be enthusiastically silent. It is not about being loud, but genuine and real. It is about authentically showing up to speak, being with your own power of expression. This is where as a presentation director I will say "go for it, don't leave anything behind, give it your all." If it is important enough to talk about, there is some room for enthusiasm, so enjoy it enthusiastically.

One of the most powerful results of giving a presentation with sincere passion and enthusiasm is the look on the faces of your listeners. They know when you are in the flow and they join you. You'll notice appreciation, surprise and genuine delight in their eyes. In today's world of advanced communication technology, there is a lack of connection and a renewed demand for person-to-person messages. After all, we're still human beings, who can speak to each other with emotion, humor and passion.

At the 1999 Academy Awards ceremony, Italian actor/director Roberto Benigni, winner of two Oscars, demonstrated what an effect authenticity, enthusiasm and joy can have upon an audience. In accepting his first award for best foreign film, he was so natural and real that, despite his limited use of English, the jaded Hollywood audience responded with loud and long applause. When he was awarded a second Oscar for best actor, Benigni leapt to his feet and started to walk on the backs of the theater chairs. By the time he got to the stage, most people in the audience were on their feet. When he finished his acceptance speech, they gave him a standing ovation!

Gwyneth Paltrow was also genuine and authentic in accepting her Oscar at the same ceremony. Her references to her grandparents struck a strong chord in the hearts of the audience. She suddenly became "real" to many who had experienced her as only an actress. In her genuine and emotive recognition of her family, Paltrow not only connected with herself and her fans but also created many new ones. As the influential American psychologist Carl Rogers reminds us, "what is most personal is also most general," yet this is often what we self-censure in our expression.

These award winners allowed themselves to show up enthusiastically and received standing ovations as a result. They were not acting; they were being authentic, genuine and real. In spite of the pressure of the event, they provided rare moments of authentic self-expression.

How to Become a Powerful Speaker

Scenario 1: *It is the night before your presentation and you have spent hours tweaking and making final touches all day, yet you are unsatisfied. As you listen to the quiet rumble of the hotel air-conditioning mixed with the sounds of traffic, you can't get to sleep. You see yourself mumbling and feeling terrified while speaking, and now you are even more awake. So you get up and look at your presentation again. It's 4 a.m., no point in trying to get back to sleep. Might as well have a coffee... Now if you only knew it would go like this...*

Scenario 2: *It is the night before your presentation and relaxed and satisfied that everything is ready, you fall into a gentle, refreshing sleep. You wake up relaxed and excited for the day ahead and for the presentation. You visualize yourself speaking well, feeling relaxed and powerful while speaking, and now you are even more energized. So you get up and get ready to have some fun while speaking.*

What follows are the tools and proven strategies to increase your performance level and to help you become a powerful speaker so that you can avoid Scenario 1 in favor of Scenario 2.

Mental & Physical Preparation

Many novice speakers overlook mental and physical preparation and spend too much time preparing the content of their presentation, using PowerPoint slides and finding the perfect word. They then arrive at the presentation, looking and feeling tired, having made changes the night before and having spent hours in front of the computer burning up their adrenal reserves. Their energy depleted, running on empty, most grab another cup of caffeine—or take an artificial relaxant or stimulant. Unfortunately, I have seen presenters and professional speakers take a stiff drink beforehand, or smoke marijuana or take cough syrup. Don't do it, you will regret your performance, or you'll never remember it! But the audience will never forgive or forget you; they have memories like a herd of elephants—and smartphones.

Rehearse? What, I Need To Rehearse?

Why rehearse? Why not just ride the adrenaline and go for it?

Let me ask you a different question: Do you want to win business, persuade others to say yes to your project, raise that seed capital? Then grow up and do the necessary work! You can't be compelling if you're worried about what you're going to say next. If you have time, review the key points you wish to make before your meeting or presentation to ensure you're versed in the topic. When there's no time to prepare, make a quick assessment of your audience and what will resonate with them. Talk about issues that matter to you.

Today's audience is sophisticated, educated and has

access to vast amounts of information. Don't give them a BS presentation; there is nowhere to hide and they have smartphones and iPads. Thanks to the Internet, they can fact-check you, review you on LinkedIn and find comments about you as you are speaking. If you are a lousy and poorly prepared speaker, they can tweet about your BS presentation in real time. The days of "fake it till you make it" are long gone, another myth busted by change.

In the Beginning

It's a good idea to plan how you will verbally emphasize key phrases and ideas, especially points that you want to repeat during your presentation. However, don't memorize specific gestures. When you've rehearsed too much, you can come across as slick and phony. It looks like you're acting rather than presenting.

The best way to prepare for delivering a presentation is with a small digital recorder. First, go over your talk without an audience, just speaking in a normal conversational voice, allowing it to be recorded. Play it back and just listen; you'll learn a lot from your first playback. You may not like the sound of your own voice (I find mine a bit weird); however, listen for the spontaneous phrases you use or any acronyms or abbreviations and decide whether they fit, and if they don't, lose them fast. On your second run-through—once you've gotten used to hearing your own voice—concentrate on staying close to your time limit and on making smooth transitions from one point to the next. On your third re-cording, have at least one person in the room. Do it standing up and speak loudly and clearly, just as you would during the actual presentation.

Recording your practice sessions is one of the most pow-erful things that you can do. Listening to your recording gives you instant feedback and immediate understanding of how you sound, and it gets you used to your own voice. However, nothing replaces a live audience (even if it is one person) listening and giving you feedback. Even then, record yourself, as you are likely to discover content changes you wish to make as you go over your talk in a practice phase. After each rehearsal, make a fresh set of notes or retype your script entirely to reflect your final version. Make clean, clear and easy-to-read notes. This will deeply ingrain your speech into your unconscious and strengthen your confidence.

Complete your final practice session at least one day before your presentation. You'll get very little benefit from last-minute practice, so relax the day before. Use the few hours before you speak, if they're available to you, to reflect on the concepts and major themes of your presentation and to visualize yourself giving your presentation successfully, with power and enthusiasm.

It's a good idea to visit the physical location of your presentation a day ahead, if you can. There is a subconscious adjustment to the exact dimensions and dynamics of the actual room in which you're going to give your speech. This will give time for your subconscious to let the environment sink in, and it will help you to visualize yourself giving your speech.

Another great way to prepare to deliver your presentation is to record yourself visually. Many people who see themselves on video before giving a business presentation are more critical of what they see than of what they hear. They tend to notice without prompting any distracting body language or gestures, uncomfortable or inhibited mannerisms and inappropriate facial expressions. The first question they usually ask is: "What do I do with my hands?" The answer is: Use your hands to make natural gestures, just as you do in a normal conversation, only make them slightly broader or bigger if you have a large audience. Small gestures appear tentative and uncertain when you're in front of a large group.

Just as we get most of our information from what we see, our strongest impression of a speaker is often the visual impression. A gesture, whether intended or not, is apt to have as great an effect on listeners as the words you are speaking. So either make relevant, productive gestures, or make none at all.

Make a Gesture, Make an Impact

Yes, wave your arms, pound on the table, raise your voice, emphasize and make an impact. Editors have highlighters. Firefighters drive big red trucks with flashing lights and sirens. They want to be seen and heard. How about you?

Being seen and heard, that's what you are supposed to be at the front of the room. So what do speakers have to emphasize the points they're trying to make? Gestures, tone of voice, volume, silence—all are available to you, every physical aspect of being human. Charisma has a physical component, so pay attention to your body language. Notice how you stand when you're feeling comfortable and in control and practice that posture. Learn to salsa dance, get some rhythm in your body, make bold gestures to emphasize your points. Become alive with energy.

When you're not using your hands to make relevant gestures or to lead the audience's attention towards visuals, keep them loosely by your sides. You may choose to put your hands in your pockets occasionally; however, don't keep them there for long, because your ability to gesture will be restricted. In addition, be sure that you've taken out any coins that might rattle in your pockets or any other items your hands might find to fidget with.

Here are some tips for using your voice and body to be a powerful speaker:

Avoid the Fig Leaf

You know, with your hands clasped in front of you. This posture tends to look defensive and gives the impression that you're apprehensive and lack certainty.

Use Your Head

From a strong nod for yes or a shake of the head to make it clear your answer is no, to the thoughtful side tilt, your head can help you emphasize your words.

Use Your Hands

Gestures not only help you speak fluently; they help your audience understand your point—even if a gesture isn't specific to the words it accompanies. Go ahead, point, stretch, glide, zoom and otherwise move around. Use your hands to emphasize what you want to say. One gesture to avoid is pointing your finger directly at a member of the audience. This feels intimidating and, to some people, quite threatening. It makes no difference that you're intending to single someone out for a friendly purpose; the effect of this particular gesture is nearly always negative. Use the open palm, point all of your fingers or your whole hand towards the individual—this gesture appears friendly and welcoming. Support your point physically at all times.

Use Your Words

Stories, after all, are but a series of words. To emphasize what you're saying, use tactics such as repetition, rhyme, alliteration, analogy and more. Use words and structure to make those big points gigantic and those small thoughts focused.

Use Your Voice

One of the easiest ways to underscore a word or phrase is with your voice. Use inflection, cadence or a pop of emphasis to make particular words stand out from the rest.

Use Your Body

Don't stay behind the lectern. When you're onstage, your body becomes one of your best tools for emphasis. When a professional speaker at one of my workshops asked, "What can I do if I think I'm losing the audience?" I walked towards him and when I reached him, I asked, "What's everyone else in the room doing right now?" He said, "Turning around to watch you." He got the point! Keep moving.

Use Pauses

Use a pause to good effect. Leaving that space after a phrase gives emphasis to what you just said and creates anticipation for what you will say next.

Use Humor

Authentic humor can engage the audience and make your point more memorable and emphatic.

Use Volume

Don't speak at one volume all the way through your presentation. You can use loudness or softness to emphasize particular points. Don't underestimate the impact of low volume; it forces the audience to lean in and listen.

Preparing your Voice

Your voice is your most powerful tool for presenting, yet many of us are unaware of what we sound like. In order to increase your awareness, make a recording of your presentation and then play it back. Listen for the following:

- *Breath: Do you run out, or do you sound tight, as if you are holding it in?*

- *Pace: Does it stay the same or does it vary?*

- *Pitch: Are you stuck in one tonal range?*

- *Volume: Do you speak too loudly or too softly?*

- *Quality: Does your voice sound thin, or does it sound rich and vibrant?*

There are four ways to vary your voice:

1. **Breath**

   Your breath is the power source for your voice. How freely you inhale and exhale dramatically affects the sound of your voice. Learning to use the diaphragm in a natural way is very important. The only muscle that is involved in producing your voice is the diaphragm. It is the accelerator that regulates the speed and amount of air you put behind your voice. Most vocal problems can be traced back to improper breathing. Use your voice like the valuable instrument it is.

2. **Pace**

   Another way to increase variety in your presentation is to play with the rhythm. Speak quickly to suggest excitement, pause for dramatic emphasis, and then speak slowly to make your point.

3. **Pitch**

Pitch helps create the richness and variety of a voice. Higher-pitched sounds are usually the result of excitement or enthusiasm. To produce lower tones, inhale deeply and, when you speak and exhale, allow the air to flow freely from your chest cavity.

4. **Volume**

How much breath you inhale and exhale determine the volume of your voice. To speak louder, exhale more fully as you speak. To speak softer, exhale slowly and with more control. Allow your diaphragm to be the accelerator that determines the amount of air and speed you put behind your voice.

Silence Is Powerful

I learned about silence from a great teacher, Dr. Woodward, when I was in drama class after school. The class was meant to help my confidence with girls—that's how Dr. W. got me to join. The language of Shakespeare had always given me fits, especially after the Romeo experience, and I was reading a passage as though it was a run-on sentence. I remember him yelling, "Breathe between the words (long deathly silence), let them make impact!" I never forgot that silence or that exclamation!

Since Dr. W.'s drama class, I've used silence in many other contexts. As a professional speaker, I have used the power of silence to make an impact and inspire audiences. Silence can be a very useful tool for sales; for example, when you're trying to close a sale, at one point you need to state your pitch, with the price, and then just shut up. If you keep talking, you will only distract the customer from the presentation and from their decision.

If you have the gift of the gab, become powerful by learning to keep your mouth shut. When you speak, punctuate your words with pauses, and when you have nothing to say, say nothing. Don't let your insecurity or need to say something important make you look foolish; learn to just shut up.

Very few people can stand the tension of silence, particularly when "I don't know what I can do to solve this" is followed by silence. This will often bring suggestions for solving the problem from the listener: "Why don't you try this?" Silence passes on many messages. One is that you are somebody with power, a person able to take a stand and wait. This demonstrates biological and physiological power: the big secure animal looking at harmless ones. Because of this, you have a better chance of being listened to when you do speak.

What to Wear

I was excited early in my speaking career because I had been booked to speak to the leaders of a very prestigious firm of insurance agents. I arrived dressed in my best suit. As it was only a short flight, I did not bring any luggage. My sponsor met me at the airport and he looked perplexed. When I asked him what was wrong, he exclaimed, "Didn't you know we are at a fishing lodge?" Sadly I did not. Fishing lodge! This was the agents' reward for being the best in the company. Now, I don't like suits that much, but I had assumed I would be speaking at a convention center, and, well, insurance agents—I had not researched my audience.

My sponsor and I looked at each other, and given that we were taking a chartered plane to the fishing lodge, I had time to go and buy what I thought was a good fit for my audience and retained my personal style. I bought jeans; a soft, relaxed shirt; a sports jacket; and some great walking boots. The presentation went well, and I came back relaxed and unshaven like everyone else. No, I didn't catch any fish, but I learned to find out a lot more about my audience before a presentation. And I still have the boots.

What you wear onstage makes an impact on the audience. They either feel you fit in and are one of them, or they feel you are different. Either way, you'll be making a definite statement about your attitude towards the subject matter and the audience. For example, in an informal retreat setting, I suggest you be relaxed. In a more formal conference setting (particularly for a first-time business presentation), I suggest you be more businesslike.

Having said that, here is a question for you: Do you want to fit in with your audience? If the answer is yes, find out what they normally wear or expect you to wear. Here is a different question: Do you want to be fully expressive, unique or authentic?" If the answer is yes, wear what makes you feel most like you.

How you dress has a big influence on how people view you and on how you view yourself. According to 99U.com, it's not about dressing in any one specific style; it's about considering your audience and using what you know about them to your advantage. Research shows that people who wear more daring outfits are perceived as more attractive and authentic, which could be advantageous for presenting to more creative industries or for making a strong impression onstage. Casual dress can also be more persuasive, depending on your audience. In 2010, a female experimenter reported that students were far more diligent in following her detailed instructions when she was dressed casually (like they were), as opposed to formal and professional.

When you're deciding on what kind of personal impact you wish to make, remember that your appearance does matter. The audience makes judgments about you, your appearance and your content of your presentation based on their personal prejudices. Sometimes you may flout convention in order to make a dramatic point, but be sure it really serves you and your message.

Before a presentation, look for and eliminate distracting aspects of your appearance. Audible distractions are the most annoying. Always empty your pockets of keys and coins. Be extra careful to remove pagers and cellular phones. Take off bracelets or other accessories that can jangle and make noise.

The eyes have it. If you wear glasses, make sure the lenses are clear and clean. Your listeners want to see your facial expressions and focus on your eyes.

Your clothing and personal appearance are ways of communicating your values, self-image and self-respect. Be aware of the messages you send. Your appearance can create a relaxed, personal environment in which the listener can easily identify with you and make an emotional connection, or it can create a substantial barrier.

Your clothing and style are an external projection of your internal authenticity, and I believe both must match. If you are uncertain about what looks good on you or what you feel comfortable in, hire a wardrobe consultant. It's a fun way to find out what works to make you look and feel more confident. This is an effective strategy for both men and women. And no matter what you choose, always show up. Personally, I am committed to being authentic in my style of clothing choice, and I like a little drama and style— that's me being me.

Do I Need a Coach?

There was a time when I needed help with a particular

presentation. My early mentor, Jim, watched, silent and blank-faced, taking notes as I spoke. My cheeks burned. What was I doing wrong? In the moment, I wished I'd never asked Jim for his help. I tried to be rational about it but failed. Because I just wanted to look cool doing it. It turned out my problem had to do with my delivery. My fellow speaker and mentor gave me some very specific feedback, and wow, it worked. What a relief that was.

It is never easy to commit to being coached, especially for those of us who believe we are well along in our careers. I'm ostensibly an expert speaker and coach. I'd finished long ago with the days of being tested and observed. I am supposed to be past needing such things. Why should I expose myself to scrutiny and possible fault-finding? Because there is always more to learn!

The moment we believe we are an "expert," we slip into what I call the "I know it" attitude. It's tough to grow and improve if you are unwilling to make a mistake and receive feedback. I take the position that I am always learning; it makes it easier to change and grow. How do I know I am still learning? By my mistakes and the risks I take.

Researchers say that elite performers and athletes must engage in "deliberate practice"—sustained, mindful efforts to develop the full range of abilities that success requires. In theory, you can do this by yourself. But most of us do not know where to start or how to proceed. Expertise requires going from unconscious incompetence to conscious incompetence to conscious competence and finally to unconscious competence. The coach provides the outside eyes and ears and makes you aware of where you're falling short and where to focus to improve.

The Day Before

I recommend that you finish your preparation and put away your presentation material twenty-four hours before the event—no exceptions. If you feel compelled to do something, study your audience—get to know them so that when you meet them, you will feel like old friends. Use your mental preparation time to get ready like an Olympic athlete, imagine doing well, seeing nods of agreement in the audience, develop a prep ritual to access the best of your abilities.

Take a day off, relax, get a massage, go for a run, go swimming, make love—take time to ready your body to support you while you deliver your presentation. Do what Michael Phelps, winner of eighteen gold and four silver medals at three Olympics, does and take a power nap and go out there full of energy. Prepare, rehearse, energize, relax and then perform!

CHAPTER 3

☄ The Arrow

In 1748, the British politician and aristocrat John Montagu, the 4th Earl of Sandwich, spent a lot of his free time playing cards, often eighteen hours a day. He greatly enjoyed eating a snack while keeping one hand free for the cards. So he came up with the idea to put beef between slices of toast, which would allow him to eat and play cards at the same time. His newly invented "sandwich" became one of the most popular snacks in the Western world. Remember, when you eat a hamburger, it's a variation of John Montagu's sandwich; perhaps McDonald's could have an Earl's Day. You will probably never again forget the story of how the sandwich was invented.

In today's fast-paced world, it is easy to believe that a single story will work for most or even all audiences. Nothing could be further from the truth. The vast diversity of our society has led to a need for every point of view to be included and recognized. This represents an enormous challenge for the speaker. In order to be heard and effective, you have to adapt to the specific needs and interests of every audience. The material must be relevant to the audience and presented in the form of a story, whether it is sixty minutes, six minutes or sixty seconds long.

This chapter is broken down into five sections.

The first section discusses the role of audience involvement and inspiration in storytelling. A story does what facts and statistics never can: it inspires and motivates. That's why effective speakers and facilitators are such expert storytellers. They can translate complex ideas into practical examples, and they know how to make emotional connections with their listeners. The real message gets through because everyone can relate to a good story. Conveying information in a story provides a rich context, remaining in the conscious memory longer and creating more memory traces.

The second section provides an overview of the creative process to help you develop and write a story, with questions to stimulate your creative mind.

The third section offers advice for writing the script for various kinds of presentations, putting pen to paper or putting words in your mouth.

The fourth section talks about the story arc. What is a story arc? Why use it? How do you use it? The five-part story structure serves as a creative guide to help integrate a story in your listener's mind.

Finally, the chapter concludes with a list of presentation don'ts to keep you on track to becoming a powerful speaker.

Tell Me a Story

Some 27,000 years ago, someone painted on a cave wall, now known as the Chauvet-Pont-d'Arc Cave, in what today is called southern France. That person was painting to tell a story. For what purpose we don't know, but we are still fascinated. These cave paintings support my belief that telling stories has been one of humankind's most fundamental communication methods throughout history.

There is a science around storytelling and how we can use it to make better decisions every day. Our brains become more active when we tell stories. We all enjoy a good story, whether it's a novel, a movie or simply an anecdote told by one of our friends. But why do we feel so much more engaged when we hear a narrative? It's in fact quite simple. If we listen to a PowerPoint presentation with boring bullet points, certain parts of the brain get activated. Scientists call these parts Broca's area and Wernicke's area. They engage the language processing functions in the brain, where we decode words into meaning. And that's it; nothing else happens.

But when we are told a story, everything can change very quickly. Not only are the language processing parts in our brain engaged, but all the other areas in our brain, that we would use when actually experiencing the events of the story, are activated, too. For example, if someone tells us about how delicious a meal was last night, our sensory cortex lights up. If the story is about the motion of driving a car, or how the baseball player threw the wicked curve ball, then our motor cortex becomes active. If we hear about a lost child, our emotional centers flare.

A story can engage the whole brain. Facts merely tell; a story engages and gives context to the facts. Stories engage us completely: emotionally, sensually and conceptually. Facts engage our thinking and our rational judgment, but without the story behind the facts, they have no context or emotional tags in the brain. Our brains are wired for storytelling. Stories live in long-term memory, whereas facts tend to live in short-term memory. Daniel Pink, author of *A Whole New Mind*, says, "Facts are widely available; it's putting them into context that makes a connection." Stories put the facts into context, fleshing out our experience and increasing retention.

When we tell stories to others who have really helped us shape our thinking and way of life, we can have the same effect on them. I believe the brains of the storyteller and of the listener can synchronize, empathize and achieve common understanding. Such is the power of story: as a social animal we love to gossip, connect and tell our stories.

More Than Facts

Facts are important; they provide information for the decision-making process. But a story is more likely to be acted upon than other means of communication. In great stories about historical heroes, they were not motivated by pure facts but by the intangible internal story behind events. Storytelling, whether in a personal or organizational setting, connects people, develops creativity and increases confidence. The use of stories in a workshop or presentation can build descriptive capabilities, increase personal and organizational learning, convey complex meaning and communicate common values and rule sets. Storytelling—story sharing, sharing history and knowledge—uses the emotive power of the human experience to bring your message to life.

I use the term "story sharing" as well as "storytelling"

to stress personalized interaction rather than performance. Description capabilities are essential in strategic thinking and planning, and create a greater awareness of what we can achieve. Fictional stories can be powerful because they provide a mechanism by which the individual or organization can learn from failure without attributing blame. Stories of personal learning are inspiring. Storytelling is a time-tested way of establishing trust and rapport, and of cementing collaborative behaviors. It's also a powerful way to transfer information and an inspiring teaching tool. The story paints a more vivid picture of the world than a column of numbers. And it does so in a way that's more likely to inspire and motivate those who hear it. In summary, storytelling is a potent transformational tool in your presentation that allows you to affect individuals and organizations.

Listening around the Fire

Stories have been told ever since humans developed language and first gathered around fire. And for a good reason: a story is not just a powerful way to impart complex information; it gives the storyteller an opportunity to build an emotional bond with the audience. Stories have helped teach, influence and bind people together, creating community. Stories have fostered the understanding—of self, of others and of life—that is vital to progress. Such understanding is sorely needed today, as we struggle to live and work together and progress towards common goals. Storytelling can be an agent for increasing employee engagement, managing change, training and development, interviewing, evaluation, operations, marketing, building corporate culture and more.

Social media relies on our innate urge to tell and be told

stories. Look at the power of Facebook. It gives us glimpses into the personal stories of our friends and family; it helps connect us. The recent popularity of infographics (depicting information, knowledge or data visually) is all about making information more interesting by making it tell a story. All great religions have at their roots powerful human stories that inspire devotion, create belief and serve as a source of cultural wisdom.

For a story to have the desired effect, it must meet certain criteria. It must be engaging and memorable. It will usually involve a measure of drama but must also be human, authentic and easy to identify with. The story must set up an unambiguous challenge, explore the actions of the audience and connect the audience's behavior to a clear outcome. Truly great stories share applicable lessons, prompt internal reflection and instigate debate among listeners.

The Creative Process

What is a story? Essentially, a story expresses how we feel about and what we do about life challenges. We all possess a time machine—it's called "story," and we activate it by writing and speaking.

Scenario: *It all begins with an ordinary day in which your life is relatively easy. You go to work day after day, and everything's fine. You like that and expect it will go on that way. But then, suddenly, changes throw your life out of whack. In one eight-hour day, you are offered a new job, a coworker and friend rushes off in hysterical panic and, on top of all that, your spouse threatens to leave you unless you come home right now.*

What will the rest of the story tell us? Will it go on to describe how, in a heroic effort to restore cosmic balance, your hopes and dreams crash around you? Then, challenged to put your life back in order, you struggle, despair and finally overcome and restore balance, learning to take nothing for granted ever again?

A good storyteller describes what it's like to deal with these challenges, calling on you to dig deeper, work with scarce resources, make difficult decisions, take action despite risks and ultimately discover the truth. Storytellers since the dawn of time, from the ancient Chinese sages and Greek playwrights through to Shakespeare and up to the present day, use this model. The hero is challenged by life and struggles to bring resolution to the challenges, conflicts and cruel reality, finally achieving wisdom and peace.

The bottom line is: What is the purpose of your story, and what do you want to achieve by telling it? Answer these questions by doing both background and content research. Research the listening audience: age, job function, cultural bias, experience, education and what they already know about what you are going to speak about. Based upon your research of the audience and their profile, redefine your purpose. Based upon your decided purpose, what is now your key message? What elements can you add from your anecdotal stories, from your professional or personal experience, or from your educational background? Research the latest technology, information or theories known about your subject matter. What are the acknowledged challenges of this industry?

Personal Stories

I have watched good friends who haven't seen each other for a while tell each other mini-stories about the challenges and changes in their lives. This is a normal human method of communicating.

When first spoken, stories are rarely sequential but are based upon the most emotional or challenging event. Rarely will a friend calmly say "at 5:18 last night I accidentally ran over my neighbor's cat." They will more likely say "God, it was a rough night. I ran over that stupid cat from next door. God, the mess was awful. He screamed, then died!"

As they say in the newsroom, if it bleeds, it leads...

The 10 Percent Rule

Use only 10 percent of your available information. The other 90 percent is for your "ground," to enhance your story, increase your focus and help refine the structure of your presentation. Your ground provides you with weight and stability as the presenter, increasing your self-confidence and strengthening your position at the front of the room.

Like an iceberg, let only 10 percent of your knowledge show:

The audience needs or wants to know: 10 percent

Your knowledge base: 100 percent

Focus on the specific needs of your audience and ask yourself what they need to hear. The audience wants to know what information you believe is relevant but not everything that you know. Less is more. Many presenters over-prepare their material, providing too much information for the listener to absorb.

This is usually because of three things:

1. *The presenter's lack of understanding of the audience.*
2. *The presenter's lack of focus and structure.*
3. *The presenter's lack of confidence.*

The Script

The most important part of any story is knowing where to start. Good stories usually include you as the hero/heroine/ organization facing challenges and change. Most signature stories show how to find creative solutions to life's challenges so that you can grow both personally and professionally. Use these stories as part of your presentations to illustrate a point or anchor a value you are espousing.

The First Draft

First drafts are never excellent, and only occasionally are they good. They are sometimes too long-winded and missing parts, for example. It's very important not to judge your writing too harshly on your first or even second draft. The idea is to be creative and let it flow.

Expect to rework your story several times before it's ready to tell, then tell it a few times, and you will soon see where it needs work. Writing is like carving a piece of stone; you need to poke away and remove any excess to reveal the beauty underneath.

A good story grows and changes, just like people. I suggest you write out the first draft in long hand, and then later you can transcribe it to your story database or word processing program for subsequent drafts. This allows you to be more free flowing and less judgmental in your writing at the outset. Just get started and let the story tell itself.

Your Best Story

Your best story is from your life. For a story to have the desired effect, it must meet certain criteria. It must be engaging and memorable. It will usually involve a measure of drama but must also be human, authentic and easy to identify with. If you tell a story from your life, at its core it must be true. It is okay to polish the story for telling but not okay to lie.

Each individual's journey is made up of significant achievements and setbacks from birth to the present. The story must identify and mark the high and low points in order of chronology, and then connect the dots to obtain a clear picture of the path their life has taken.

The act of plotting your journey requires careful consideration and often leads to deep reflection about the events that have influenced and shaped your sense of self. Significant life events may include managing a paper route at thirteen, losing a beloved parent or grandparent, saving up to buy a car, getting promoted or fired, getting married or divorced, having or losing a baby. These are the beginnings of wonderful, rich stories that can inspire, motivate and influence others.

After plotting your story, share it with your team. Then listen to other people's stories and discuss what you and they heard and provide feedback. Does your story represent your values, principles and expectations? Could your team connect the story to a real-life challenge? Practice telling your story and identify instances where you could use this story to exemplify a principle or illustrate a point of view.

Opening Remarks

You have about three to five minutes to convince the audience that you've got something interesting to say. Find an engaging opening statement or a compelling first sentence. A good source is *Peter's Quotations* by Lawrence Peter.

If you are introducing yourself, you may give the audience a brief background about your experience or why you are the relevant speaker for the subject or what the benefit will be from listening to you as you speak about the topic. Avoid introducing yourself with a long-winded biography or résumé, as you can be perceived as being egoistical or self-indulgent. Always focus your opening remarks on the subject matter at hand and the interests of the audience.

Make your opening statement relate to your business point of view, not to the audience or the city where you're speaking—that may be appropriate for the middle of your talk, but you've been asked to speak because you're an expert on a business topic, so start on a businesslike note.

Unless you've set it up as a thought-provoking rhetorical question for your audience and you know in advance what the response will be, avoid asking a question as an opener. Otherwise, you risk soliciting offbeat, off target, irrelevant and distracting comments or reactions from the audience.

Unless it is a formal occasion, you don't have to thank the person introducing you or thank the audience for coming. That often seems insincere. It will be a pleasant surprise for your listeners if you jump right in to your powerful opening sentence. This will automatically identify you as a no-nonsense, passionate and compelling speaker.

Pause before you open your mouth to speak. Focus your eyes on one person in the audience, preferably someone about halfway to the back or in the first ten rows. You will automatically speak louder than if you looked at somebody in the front row.

Don't compromise the impact of your planned opening statement by trying to respond to the remarks of the previous speaker. Stay on track. It is a better plan to stick with your rehearsed opening, no matter how tempting it might be to change it.

Using Metaphors as Shortcuts

Some people think of metaphors as nothing more than the sweet stuff of songs and poems: love is a jewel, or a rose, or a butterfly. But, in fact, all of us speak and write and think in metaphors every day. We can't avoid them; metaphors are built right into our language. For example: "The singer had a velvet voice" or "He had leathery hands" or "Her eyes smiled with love" or "The buck stops here." We use them to convey meaning quickly, acting like shortcuts or links on a web page, and they provide deeper context.

When the character Dr. House in the TV series *House M.D.* says, "I'm a night owl; Wilson's an early bird. We're different species," he's speaking metaphorically. When Dr. Cuddy replies, "Then move him into his own cage," she's extending House's bird metaphor—which he caps off with the remark "Who'll clean the droppings from mine?"

The term "metaphor" means in ancient Greek "carry something across" or "transfer," which applies to the more elaborate definitions below:

- *A comparison between two things, based on resemblance or similarity, without using "like" or "as."*

- *The act of giving a thing a name that belongs to something else.*

- I particularly like the Greek philosopher Diomedes's definition: *a device for seeing something in terms of something else.*

Related terms

Extended or telescoping metaphor, or a sustained metaphor
"The teacher descended upon the exams, sank his talons into their pages, ripped the answers to shreds and then, perching in his chair, began to digest."

Implied metaphor, which is a less direct metaphor
"John swelled and ruffled his plumage." (Instead of "John was a peacock.")

Mixed metaphor, which is the awkward, often silly, use of more than one metaphor at a time. To be avoided!
"The movie struck a spark that massaged the audience's conscience."

Dead metaphor, which is a commonly used metaphor that has over time become part of ordinary language
Tying up loose ends, a submarine sandwich, a branch of government, a slippery slope, military intelligence—these are now clichés.

Incorporating Humor

The most natural expression of humor is the smile, and since most smiles are started by other smiles, simply make it a point to smile at least a couple of times during your talk—especially at the beginning. By relaxing, you'll naturally be more humorous. Don't worry about deliberately incorporating humor. Most speakers can find something that is naturally funny to laugh at during a talk, such as an upside-down slide, a Freudian slip or even forgetting your own name, or something humorous that members of the audience throw in, intentionally or not, during a Q&A period. The point is: don't take yourself too seriously; your natural sense of humor will come through in your presentation if you're relaxed.

What about jokes? Being a stand-up comedian is an art mastered by only a few lifetime professionals. If you're not one of them, why risk making a fool of yourself in the attempt? My advice is, don't do it, don't tell jokes. If you feel you must tell a joke, try it out on a couple of associates who not only know the audience you plan to use it on but also know you well enough to tell you if it's not appropriate for the occasion. Or if it's not funny.

Instead of jokes, amusing incidents and stories from real life are sometimes quite appropriate and effective. The key is timing. Tell the story at the right point in your talk, tie it into the theme of your presentation and tell it briefly. Take an improvisational comedy class if you want to learn to tell quick, funny stories. You will learn a great deal about how stories can come together in an instant.

If you choose to use humor in your presentation, here are some guidelines:

- *Your humor should always be appropriate and relevant to your point of view.*

- *Always balance your professionalism with your humanness.*

- *Use your own personal stories, observations or humorous asides for a lighthearted approach. Laugh at yourself and enjoy it with the audience.*

- *Humor should only be directed at yourself. Be aware of any slang or colloquialism that might be offensive.*

- *Never use a member of the audience as the butt of a joke.*

Introducing Another Speaker

Before you start to write the introduction, check with the speaker, because many have written an introduction that they prefer. I have been poorly introduced so often that I now send one in advance, then check with the person who is going to introduce me to find out how they feel about it and whether it fits the audience. If you don't receive this advance information or support and you don't know the person, interview him or her by phone to get some additional interesting material. Always double-check your information—résumés and newspaper clippings—because facts change: people change job titles and affiliations, gain new resources and create new headlines.

The key to an effective introduction is to give the audience a logical reason why the speaker was asked to be there. This usually has nothing to do with where he or she went to school or how many kids they've got. Tell the audience that they're about to hear from an expert and then relay the information that makes the speaker the expert (i.e., their qualifications and how much experience they have). The major exceptions to the logical reason rule are testimonial introductions and award introductions. In these cases, where the honorary or recipient is going to give an acceptance speech, the introduction is a mini-speech itself. Your best plan is to get a detailed résumé from the individual. Then if you don't know the person, interview him or her by phone to get some additional interesting material. Even better, interview one or two of the person's acquaintances and build a personal profile, because a testimonial refers to the character and qualities of the person you're introducing. Again, double-check information in résumés and newspaper clippings, because facts change.

Don't say, "Our guest speaker needs no introduction." This is foolish, as you're there to do an introduction. Be different. Come right out with the speaker's name: "Mary Smith is not only a key executive of ____, she is a leading authority on ____." Everybody knows her name (usually there is a printed program), so why pretend you're building to a surprise by waiting until the end of the introduction to give the speaker's name? Say it out loud, say it up front and go from there.

If you're introducing someone who's well known to most of the attendees, such as a fellow executive in the same company, use the opportunity to say something new about him or her. Part of your job is to get the speaker off to a good start, and even old friends appreciate thoughtful introductions.

Team Presentations

The analogy of a relay race is an apt illustration of how team presentations can work. Each member of the team has a leg of the race to run, but all the members train at the same time. The most important part of the relay race is the hand-off; it must occur easily and seamlessly, for if anyone drops the baton, the race is lost. If someone does not keep up with the competition, the race is also lost.

Remember, any time you get up to do a presentation as a team, each member's performance affects the end result, and in order to become a more effective team, you must help each other, coach each other and use your individual strengths to win the race. Before any race, there is tension, even anxiety, about performing well. Practice helps to create the state of mind necessary to succeed.

The greatest challenge is to become a true team, not merely a group of individuals, by using the talents and resources of each other to create an effective presentation. This means putting aside any competitiveness between team members, because the audience is more important than any single person. When you take the time to practice together, you learn how to support each other. Most executives are unwilling to admit that they award funding or support to those who demonstrate confidence, knowledge and belief in what they are presenting. The decision is more about feel than logic, more about a sense that the team is committed to what they are proposing before, during and after the presentation.

Passing the baton on to the next member in a team presentation means introducing them and in essence "selling" them to your listening audience. When you have finished your piece, always wait for your team member to join you at the front of the room, just as you would wait to pass the baton in a race. Assign time limits to each segment and respect each other's time. Stay on time and do not go over. That is a sign of lack of rehearsal. Practice together so that you will look good, sound good and understand each other's presentation and reasoning.

In a typical business presentation, questions are solicited from the audience by the last speaker but answered by the most appropriate team member. Decide who will answer which questions based on the team member who presented that section and who has the knowledge or expertise in that area. Play devil's advocate for each other. Write a series of simulated audience questions before the rehearsal. This will teach you to think on your feet and help to clarify your presentation.

The Dreaded Q&A

Keep calm and carry on. It is important to remember that the question and answer session is part of your presentation and to prepare accordingly. Questions often arise when someone does not understand or believe what you have said and they are looking for reassurance from your answers. The questions give you an opportunity to reinforce points from your presentation. Your skill at handling the question and answer period is vital to the success of your presentation.

When I coach teams involved in business presentations, I create a mock panel of experts to ask difficult questions. This reveals how well the team is prepared and whether more coaching is needed. This tactic was integral to the success in winning the Olympic bid.

Sometimes the hardest part of a Q&A is getting people to ask questions. This is especially true with large audiences, because no one wants to be first. Break the ice by asking a rhetorical question related to your subject. Once the first person speaks, other questions will follow.

Unless you want to be interrupted in the middle of your talk, let the audience know in advance that you are saving plenty of time for questions at the end, and ask them to hold their questions until that time.

With audiences of thirty or more people, it is a good idea to repeat each question so that the entire audience can hear. This also gives you valuable thinking time.

Never say "good question," for what you mean is "I have a great answer." If you don't respond with "good question" each time, the questioner you forgot to say it to will feel insulted. When it is truly a difficult question, your mind is busy trying to answer and you will forget to say "good question." Just say "thank you for your question."

Do not change the contextual or emotional meaning of a question. If you do, it will be interpreted that you are unwilling or unable to answer the question. Always repeat it aloud as asked. Always look directly at the person asking you a question and make sure they are finished before you start your answer. But during your answer, do not look at the questioner, but talk to the whole audience. If you direct your response only to the questioner, you will lose the audience's attention. Once you have finished responding, do not ask the questioner whether their question has been answered. It probably hasn't, but the rest of the audience doesn't care, so why start a detailed discussion with one person? Keep things moving and go on to the next question or questioner.

What if a previous questioner comes back for a more thorough answer? Offer to spend some extra time after the presentation just for them. Remember to acknowledge how important they are to you.

If it's your client or boss asking you a question, you must already know the answer! If it's a nitpicker, or someone wanting to make a point or look good, be polite, give some additional information, but don't get bogged down. If they persist, tell them you'll be happy to meet with them afterwards for a longer discussion of that specific point.

Let the audience know when you're wrapping up by announcing that you have time for only one more question. Be specific. If you intend to take two or more, tell them, but don't say "one or two more"—that sounds indecisive.

The Story Arc

The Five Cs of Story Structure

The five-C story structure serves as a creative guide and helps to integrate your story in your listener's mind. Using this structure will also help you craft a story quickly. As a starting point, imagine telling your best friend a story. Write down the story, using the five Cs listed below:

1. Context
The background for the rest of the story to make sense. Establish the present situation or status quo. This leads the listener into and creates a context for Parts 2, 3 and 4.

2. Challenge
The challenge/problem to be overcome. Bring in a new element so that the hero must make a new decision or discovery, or encounter conflict or trouble.

3. Choices
The actions taken to find a solution. What happens as a result of this new challenge in the hero's life, what is different, what is challenging and potentially dangerous?

4. Consequences
The consequences of the action taken. How does the hero

deal with those consequences? Do the solutions work? This usually involves the hero encountering many obstacles and trying many things before actually finding the one that works. Overcoming these obstacles, however, involves both small and big heroic acts. And they require the hero to act outside of his or her comfort zone, be bold, courageous and creative, and try something new.

5. Conclusion

The final result and the new reality. The new status quo or how the story has changed the hero.

The Five-C Story Structure: James Bond

The following is an example of how the five-C story structure applies to a well-known movie story: the newest James Bond film, *Skyfall*.

1. Context

In *Skyfall*, Bond finds a fellow agent dying. He pursues the killer, but while trying to recover the stolen disc he is shot by another MI5 agent and is presumed dead. He survives, damaged and emotionally torn, and drinks heavily. This sets the scene for the next act.

2. Challenge

After leaving Bond's funeral service, M watches MI5 headquarters breached and blown up. Bond, curing a hangover, sees the news story on TV and decides to return from the dead to help. Bond discovers all his belongings have been sold. Now the action starts!

3. Choices
MI5 demands Bond pass a physical. Bond discovers MI5 and M have a new tough boss. Bond goes looking for the villain.

4. Consequences
Bond finds the killer and takes his special coin. Then he encounters a beautiful girl and claims a fortune. The girl leads Bond to the real villain, and Bond brings this villain back to MI5. The villain uses this as an opportunity to launch his attack on MI5 and M. Bond takes M to Skyfall and prepares for a final showdown with the villain. Bond kills the villain, but M dies in his arms.

5. Conclusion
Bond has lost his dear friend M and now has a new boss. Our wounded hero is ready for more adventures...

The Five-C Story Structure: Apple
The following is an example of how the five-C story structure applies to a well-known business story: the rise of Apple and Steve Jobs as CEO and founder. In this example, I use a timeline to define the events.

1. Context
Steve Jobs was an American entrepreneur, the cofounder and later the chairman and CEO of Apple Inc. Apple was founded on April 1, 1976.

2. Challenge
After a power struggle with the Apple board of directors in 1985, Jobs left Apple. Was he fired or did he quit?

3. Choices:
At loose ends in 1985, Jobs underwent a time of personal reflection and change. He loved Apple and missed it! He took action to prove his worth. Jobs founded NeXT, a computer platform development company specializing in the higher-education and business markets. In 1986, he acquired the computer graphics division of Lucasfilm, which later spun off as Pixar. He was credited as an executive producer in *Toy Story*.

4. Consequences
In 1996, Jobs returned to Apple as an advisor and took control of the company as interim CEO. By 1998, he brought Apple back from near bankruptcy to profitability, and the business story continued. In 2003, Jobs was diagnosed with pancreatic cancer.

5. Conclusion
In his final years, it is said that Jobs desired for the truth to be told about his life, so he had a biography written by Walter Isaacson. However, his drive to see Apple grow continued to the very end. Through his work at Apple, he was widely recognized as a charismatic pioneer of the personal computer revolution and for his influential career in the computer and consumer electronics fields. He died in 2011.

The Five-C Story Structure: Rocky Mountaineer
The following is a business presentation using the five-C story structure. In 2004, Rocky Mountaineer president Peter Armstrong contacted me with the challenge to help the company tell its story in a presentation to win a bid to use the Vancouver/Whistler rail line as a passenger and tour-

ist attraction, creating a destination "rail-tour." Originally, negotiations with B.C. Rail were going well, local people talking with local people. Then the B.C. government sold the transportation rights to the Canadian National Railway Company. Suddenly, the contract became an open public tender and many other companies joined the competition. Our challenge was to establish credibility with a large international railroad, one of the largest in North America. We needed to tell our story as successful rail-tour operators.

I. Context

We set the stage for CN with the message: "We believe our experience and resources will lead to success." Then we ran a three-minute special infomercial video showing the fabulous railcars and food service, and lots of happy passengers. We established ourselves as a successful rail-tour company that moves people, not grain, coal or other goods. This gave CN the background information that Rocky Mountaineer was operational and successful.

2. Challenge

We described the challenge of the many failed rail-tour projects around the world. We had some great stories to tell, with visuals. This gave us the opportunity to position our competitors in the one group, as they did not have any railcars or active rail-tour service. In other words, they were not railroaders.

3. Choices

We then told the story of Rocky Mountaineer's start-up challenges and problems and how they were solved. By describing what we learned and why we were successful, we established operational credibility in the minds of the CN audience.

4. Consequences

We understood freight trains to be the lifeblood of CN. We then told the story of Rocky Mountaineer successes, using examples of how as railroaders we would ensure what we had learned would be applied to working with CN.

5. Conclusion

Our concluding message in our pitch to CN was: "We have a vision, and here is what we plan to do next. We are committed to creating a long-term, viable rail-tour service, and we know how to do it. We would like to have the right to include the Vancouver/Whistler line in it." We won and today the route is called the Whistler Sea to Sky Climb.

A Short Story

The following story employs all of the five Cs of story structure. Read the story and try to identify them.

A Samurai general once went to see a monk. "Monk," he said, in a voice accustomed to instant obedience, "teach me about heaven and hell!"

The monk looked up at this mighty warrior and replied with disdain, "Teach you about heaven and hell? I couldn't teach you about anything. You're dirty. You smell. Your blade is rusty. You're a disgrace and an embarrassment to the Samurai class. Get out of my sight. I can't stand you."

The Samurai general was furious. He shook, red in the face, speechless with maniacal rage. He pulled out his sword and raised it above him, preparing to behead the monk.

"That's hell," said the monk softly.

The general was instantly overwhelmed by the compassion and surrender of this little man who had offered his life to give this teaching to show him hell. He slowly put down his sword,

filled with gratitude and suddenly peaceful.
    "And that is heaven," said the monk softly.

What impact did this story have on you? How did it make you feel? What did it make you think? As you can see, a story doesn't need to be long or involved to have a profound effect on an audience. Here, I have identified the five Cs:

1. Context
A samurai general once went to see a monk. "Monk," he said, in a voice accustomed to instant obedience.

2. Challenge
"Teach me about heaven and hell!"

3. Choice
The monk looked up at this mighty warrior and replied with disdain, "Teach you about heaven and hell? I couldn't teach you about anything. You're dirty. You smell. Your blade is rusty. You're a disgrace and an embarrassment to the samurai class. Get out of my sight. I can't stand you."

4. Consequences
The samurai general was furious. He shook, red in the face, speechless with maniacal rage. He pulled out his sword and raised it above him, preparing to behead the monk.
"That's hell," said the monk softly.
    The general was instantly overwhelmed by the compassion and surrender of this little man who had offered his life to give this teaching to show him hell. He slowly put down his sword, filled with gratitude and suddenly peaceful.

5. Conclusion:
"And that is heaven," said the monk softly.

Ten Questions

Here are ten questions to help you build your story outline:

1. What is the initial status quo? Where does the story start? Who, what, where, when and why?

2. What is the moment of conflict, challenge, change, decision or discovery? Write it as succinctly as possible. If there were many, pick the most dramatic one. This is usually a life-changing event, such as losing money, a job, relationships or health. Another way to look at it is as a time when you changed your sense of identity or lost a sense of security, control, approval or connection with life.

3. What are the consequences of this change or challenge? This is the chaos phase in which you try to regain stability. Where did you end up, how did you feel, what problems did it cause, what were the new elements you had to contend with, what was now missing from your life or what was now added to your life?

4. How did you deal with the change and regain stability, balance, flow or a sense of connection? What kinds of obstacles did you face and how did you approach them? What did you have to do in order to finally succeed?

5. The new status quo. How did you change as a result of this experience, what did you learn, how did you grow as a person, what set of character traits or sense of identity did it build and what were your new life circumstances?

6. What kinds of values are at the core of this story? What is the theme, or what is this story really all about? Think of words such as "balance," "compassion," "self-acceptance," "courage," "wisdom," "forgiveness," "stepping into the unknown" and "believing in yourself."

7. When in history did this happen? For example, the 1940s, five years ago, just yesterday?

8. What sights, smells, sounds, feelings and tastes can you describe in the story? Create a connection to the senses.

9. What act-outs can you do? These are ways to portray the characters and their actions in the story. In other words, how can you physicalize and vocalize the story?

10. How can you end the story? This could take the form of a quotation, a "bookend," a visual image or a verbal punctuation.

Presentation Don'ts

Don't speak about religion and politics unless they are the topic of your presentation. And don't ever use off-color material or four-letter words in a business presentation. This is not prudish but rather a basic principle of good business communication. The exception to this rule is when you want to deliberately emotionally upset and challenge your audience. Be ready to follow up when you have their attention, and whatever you do, don't hesitate or flinch, because then all will be lost. I once saw a petite, pretty, young female presenter use the

F-bomb with amazing results. Be ready for the audience re-action.

Don't ever accept a speaking assignment that you don't have time to prepare for. It's possible to speak about practically any subject if you have time to prepare—or at least you can talk about what you know about the subject in an interesting manner. However, experts who are not prepared to speak give the most disastrous presentations.

Don't ever attempt to answer a question if you don't know the answer. Although spontaneous answers to routine questions are not expected to be perfect, any suggestion of fabrication will destroy your credibility. When you get a tough question that you can't answer, say so and add confidently that you will get the information to the questioner and anyone else who's interested. (For sales and marketing executives, this is a perfect excuse for a follow-up contact.)

Don't ever call upon an associate or a colleague in an audience to answer a question you can't handle, unless he or she has given you previous permission and has agreed to be available for that purpose.

Don't ever lose your temper before an audience, even if a rude heckler provokes you. An attack on one member of the audience is perceived as an attack upon all. Stay calm, let the heckler attack you and the audience will move to your side.

Don't ever forget that you're talking to real, live human beings just like yourself. They don't expect you to be perfect any more than you expect perfection from other speakers. What most business people are looking for is honest, easy-to-understand conversation, delivered clearly and concisely.

CHAPTER 4

⤜ The Bow

The bow represents the delivery system for the story to be conveyed to the audience. What is the most effective media through which to deliver the story? Is it PowerPoint slides, handouts, a flip chart, audiovisuals or even direct access to a website? The tools selected must fit the message, the venue and the audience.

This chapter is divided into three sections.

The first section addresses the old-school style of "pure logic" presentations and recommends alternative strategies that engage the emotions to more effectively communicate with the audience.

The second section presents a selection of the available presentation tools and resources at your disposal.

And the third section is a handy presentation checklist.

Are You Bored with Pure Logic?

If you are using an old-fashioned "pure logic" presentation style, then what you do now is boring and ineffective. It doesn't engage the audience. As you make presentations in the future, instead of making slides that follow your pure logic–driven bullet points, organize the presentation emotionally, letting the full message drive the process. Remember that every slide does not have to stand on its own. You can use one slide to set up a point and then the next slide to bring it home.

Let's say you work for a nonprofit and are doing a presentation for your backers at the Children's Hospital. You want more money for a program that helps parents get the support and therapy they need as they cope with a terribly ill child, perhaps as they prepare for their child's death.

Using the old way of pure logic, you might start with a bar chart about the financial and social impact facing a family and then follow that with five bullet points about how you'll approach the problem.

For a more innovative presentation, ask the audience to imagine these images: a small healthy child being cuddled by a happy parent, followed by a small sick child being cuddled by a worried parent. Then while the audience grasps the feelings and memories these images bring forth, tell your story. Tell it the way you'd tell a friend. Explain why you want to support and help this program and whom it is going to benefit. Then refer your audience to the facts and figures you'll be happy to hand out in a few minutes. Show more digital images of the people already in the program. Insert a few photos of well children and happy families now leading productive lives with the organization's help.

Here's a simpler example: you want to convince your boss to approve a budget to redesign your website. Your competition is gaining ground because your site is so ineffective and hard to use. Instead of regaling your boss with statistics, show them the problem.

Create ten screen shots, one after another, demonstrating the process of buying products online from your website. Then show the three steps it takes your competitor's customers. It will only take you thirty seconds to work through the steps, but once you're done, you've established a real need for your boss to authorize the new website budget.

Define and show the problem and it's easier to sell the solution. Because your presentation is for a project approval, use an instant feedback cycle. Hand your boss a project approval form before you start and get them to approve it upon completion, just so that there's no ambiguity about what's been agreed to or the purpose of your presentation. You will also discover—very quickly—whether you have done a good job of presenting to and persuading your boss.

The strategies I've just described are simple and effective, yet difficult for most people to grasp because they think people are rational and driven by pure logic. Nobody is motivated by pure logic or by pure emotion; in fact, we are very complex, and most people make decisions and commitments based on a combination of reason and emotion. Most of us see something we like and want, and then use our rational mind to justify why we must have it. I love hi-tech electronics, and I have been reading that Apple has a new MacPro coming very soon. I want it and, oh yes, I have a list of reasons to justify the purchase already.

The purpose of any presentation software is to help you communicate with your audience. Unfortunately, rather than communicating, it is often used to accomplish four other things, none of which leads to a good presentation or powerful results.

The first thing that most people use presentation software for is as a teleprompter. Did your audience really have to come all this way to listen to you read the slides? The last person who read to me was my mother and she was attempting to put me to sleep. Why not just send the audience the presentation before the meeting, as it is obvious you're not needed?

The second is to provide a written record of what was presented. And by handing out the slides after the meeting or, much worse, before, the presenter is avoiding the job of writing a formal report—tacky, lazy and tacky—and is covertly seeking implicit approval for what is said at the meeting.

The third purpose is to make it easier for the audience to remember everything you said. Sort of like reading your slides—but better? After all, if you read your slides, and then give the audience a verbatim transcript of what you read, what could be wrong with that? Oh, so very much.

The fourth is to impress the audience with the depth and complexity of the presentation. It is a monumental data dump that gives everyone a headache and causes more confusion and questions, but at least it is impressive in its size. So is the run on Tylenol afterwards.

The E-Factor

If all you do is create a presentation of facts and figures, cancel the meeting and send a report. Do it in any program you want, but it's not a presentation; it's a report. It will contain whatever you write down, but don't imagine for a second that you're powerfully communicating your ideas or your commitment. Facts tell; emotional connection sells.

Communication is about getting others involved in your point of view, helping them understand why you're excited (or sad or optimistic or whatever else you are). It's awfully hard to do that in a report—unless you're an amazing writer. What most people set out to do with presentation software is in direct conflict with what a great presentation can and should do.

Our brains have two sides. The right side is emotional, musical and moody. The left side is focused on dexterity, facts and hard data. Engage the two sides of the brain to make an impact. When you give a presentation, people want you to engage both parts of their brain. If you don't, they will use the right side to judge the way you talk, the way you dress and your body language. Often, people come to a conclusion about your presentation by the time you're on the second or third slide. After that, it's too late for your bullet points to do much good.

You can wreck a communication process with lousy logic or unsupported facts, but you can't complete it without emotion—the E-factor. Logic is not enough. If all it took was pure logic, no one would smoke cigarettes or drive drunk. If pure logic applied, then every smart proposal would be adopted. The world, however, is full of hopes and fears. Yes, logic is essential, but without emotion, you're not using the full range and expression of human communication.

Visual software platforms present an amazing opportunity. You can use the screen to connect emotionally to the audience's right brain (through their eyes), and your words can connect to their left brain (through their ears). You put up a slide with an evocative image and it triggers an emotional response in the audience. They want to know what you're going to say that fits with that image. Then, if you do it right, every time they think of what you said, they'll see the image and experience what you mean as well as hear it. Make slides that reinforce your words, not repeat them verbatim. Create slides that demonstrate your point of view, not just factually but with emotional proof that what you're saying is true.

Images make the difference. Talking about pollution? Instead of just giving me four bullet points of data, why not show me a photo of a sick tree, smog or the diseased lungs of a child? It's more powerful than doing it the old way, and it's effective human communication—using right and left brain communications at the same time.

Create a written document, using as many footnotes or details as you like (in the presentation program itself). Then, when you start your presentation, tell the audience that you're going to give them all the details of your presentation after it's over, and they don't have to write down everything you say; they can then focus on you. This way, your presentation will get them to sit back, trust you and take in the emotional and intellectual points.

You Are Selling

If everyone in the room agreed with you just because you were there, you wouldn't need to make a presentation! You could just hand out a one-page project report to each person. The reason we do presentations is to make a point, to sell ideas. But most people think selling is hard and don't want to admit that they're selling. This is another myth I want to bust, but that's another book.

Be different and sell to your audience. Make sure your presentations are not boring—present with some enthusiasm. Otherwise, it's a waste of time and energy for them and for you. If you believe in your idea, sell it. Make your point as hard as you can and get what you came for. Your audience will thank you for it, because deep down, we all want to be sold.

What's On Your Slides?

Here are the five rules for creating amazing presentations:

1. No more than three points on a slide. And no more than six words per point.

2. No slick or cheesy images. Instead, use images from one of the professional providers—at last count, there were thousands on the Internet. They cost as little as $3 each, or a little more if they're for professional use.

3. No razzle-dazzle 'em or psychedelic effects in a business presentation. No dissolves, spins or other transitions.

4. Use sound effects judicially and sparingly. Only use sound effects a few times per presentation, but never use the sound effects that are built in to the program. Instead, leverage the emotional impact of sound and music by using CDs or music downloaded from the Internet. Remember to pay the copyright if it is a repetitive public presentation.

5. Don't provide printouts of your slides. Printouts are one dimensional, flat and often printed only in black and white. They are not emotive, and they don't work without you there.

Presentation Tools & Resources

As most business presentations today have audiences of ten to twenty-five people, you will need to choose your audiovisual aids according to your environment. If you are speaking in a large auditorium or convention center, you will have access to many of the following tools, and often the organizer will ask you for your presentation in advance so that they can load it into their system. Always find out beforehand whether this will be possible.

The following is a list of some of the tools to consider:

Room Setup
Although it is often overlooked for small meetings, the setting, including the sight lines, chairs and colors, affects the audience. Flowers always relax the audience, and so do place cards with names on them. A relaxed audience listens better.

Flip Charts
These have improved greatly, from butcher wrapping paper to now 3M's bleed-proof flip chart that is like a giant sticky note. It never leaves marks on the wall and won't allow the pen ink to bleed through.

Video or Audio Clips
Insert them into your software presentation—you can even use a live link.

Animation
It is becoming affordable and can help tell your story.

Webinars

There are some amazing platforms available that allow clarity of presentation and engagement with the audience.

Wireless Microphone

It can be connected to a public address system or soundboard to modulate the tone and pitch of your voice.

Projectors

There are now high-intensity projectors so small they can fit inside a briefcase.

Giant Screens

Soon, wall-sized screens will be an option.

iPads or Tablets

You might have one for yourself or one for each audience member. Tablets have enormous potential to engage and mesmerize the user. Just lock the tablet in presentation mode while you're speaking and then let the audience play afterwards. The TouchCast platform is well suited to iPads or other tablets and is a great presentation tool with amazing flexibility.

Models or Replicas

These are often forgotten, but they can be very powerful in small groups for demonstrating architecture. Three-dimensional printing of a prototype is now affordable and widely available.

Your Natural Voice

Hire a voice coach and learn how to project and stage whisper.

Your Appearance

Dress to fit in and belong or dress for dramatic effect to sep-
arate yourself from the audience. Choose a natural look or
wear makeup.

Room Setup

Arrive early and check out the room setup. Most convention
facilities will make the extra effort to rearrange the setup
to suit your needs. Better still, let the facility know in advance the setup you would prefer. Be ready for last-minute
changes to your plans. If you are going to a client's facility,
ask about the room layout ahead of time and request your
preferred setup so that you can deliver a top-quality presentation.

Hotels vs. Presentations

When booking a presentation at a hotel it would be natural
to assume that the hotel staff is working for you. Well, that
is not exactly the case. Yes, you pay the bill and they want to
maximize their profit from your event.

The banquet table—you know, the hated round table for
ten—makes it difficult to connect. You can't reach over and
shake hands or exchange business cards or talk with all the
people you hoped to meet. And if you speak to the person on
one side you have to ignore the person on the other.

But this table allows the hotel room for flowers, bread
baskets and water, so they will assume you want it or will
nudge you towards it, because it makes life easier for them.
It is the perfect size for the kitchen and the servers...

The fact is that half of your guests will have their backs
towards your presentation and if they turn around, they
have no convenient place to put notebooks or coffee cups.

It's convenient for the hotel, but absolutely NOT for you, the presenter. In fact, it's the worst possible seating for your presentation.

Having attended thousands of events and spoken at even more, I can tell you that the single worst thing an organizer can do is sit people at tables for ten. Be careful if you let the banquet manager run your next event; understand that his goals are different from yours, even if you are paying the bill.

Flip Chart Dos & Don'ts

As a workshop leader, I have used flip charts to involve and inform my participants. Flip charts are one of the most versatile tools available to speakers.

Here are few tips:

Check and double-check that you have markers (and that they aren't dried out) and enough paper. I like to use 3M paper, as it has an adhesive bar on the back that makes it easy to stick to the walls without damaging them. It also has faint blue lines, which help my printing stay straight. I once used another product and wrote on the paper while it was hanging on the wall, only to find that the ink had bled through. It cost more than my fee to repaint that boardroom.

I like to use dark colors, as this maximizes visibility to the back of the room. Your best bet is to stick to high-contrast colors such as black, blue, red or dark green. Stay away from yellow or pastels; they are too hard to see. If you are using more than one color, use them consistently. I typically use black as my base color and red or blue to emphasize key words.

Position the flip chart where it has light upon it and where people can see it. Before the presentation, I will sit in different spots in the room to check visibility for the audience. Lots of people advise standing to the side, even when writing. I can't do this and have my writing be legible, so it is important to quickly move off to the side when you've finished writing or drawing to avoid being an obstacle.

Don't write; print and print large, so that the back row can read it. Practice printing and become good at it. If nobody can read what you've written, what's the point?

Focus on single words or short phrases and use bullet points. Flip charts are good for planned diagrams, but they really shine when used for impromptu sketches. Use colors wisely.

Sketch diagrams in pencil beforehand, and nobody will be able to see them. Then, during your session, just draw over these invisible lines with markers. I like to do this because I am not good at sketching; however, I let the audience in on what I am doing, using it as a teaching moment.

Reconnect your audience to previous ideas or concepts by referring back to relevant flip chart pages from earlier in your presentation. I refer to those questions as they are answered and rip off the pages and post them on the wall to ensure they are accessible.

Audiovisual Tools

In the last few years there has been an explosion of new software presentation tools to challenge the passivity of PowerPoint.

According to the marketing software platform HubSpot,

90 percent of information transmitted to the brain is based on visuals. This by far beats out other cues such as touch, smell and sound. So although a well-delivered speech or an artfully crafted podcast can be helpful additions to a presentation, neither engages your audience's primary means of absorbing data.

A video presentation can enrich your message and truly capture the audience's attention by providing the visual elements needed to make you memorable. Whether you are giving the keynote address at an event, pitching to potential business partners or virtually presenting your company's core values, a video can add that little something extra to your delivery.

But aside from the everyday PowerPoint, where do you begin when creating a visual display to support your presentation, product or service?

If you want to bolster your business message but don't have a lot of video experience, here are several different video presentation software platforms that can make the production process easier.

Prezi

Prezi is about as different from PowerPoint as you can get. Rather than a slide-by-slide presentation, it's more of a visual and interactive mind map, wherein you interact with different elements on a virtual canvas. You can convert your PowerPoint presentation slides into a dynamic user experience or create a brand new Prezi from scratch.

Prezi is an online tool, so it's available anywhere with an Internet connection. There's also the ability to work offline and to set security levels around who can see your animated presentations. Because Prezi is nonlinear, it's easy to jump from editing one part to another, though this can be difficult to get used to at first. Once you're done, publish the presentation on Prezi.com or embed it on your own website.

GoAnimate

In many cases, an informative, animated video presentation is the best way to get your message across. Although it's not strictly business presentation software, GoAnimate provides you with the tools to create a standout animation so that you can focus on your narrative. It's a full suite of applications designed to help users create animated presentations for free.

GoAnimate is a great platform for presenting your ideas, with a huge variety of premade themes, props and characters tailored for making professional business presentations. Rather than just queuing up images in slides, you can produce a professional-looking video from scratch in minutes—without drawing anything or operating a camera. Just drag and drop from the extensive content library and forget about recording or editing. Then download, share or publish your finished animated presentation to YouTube.

SlideRocket

Now we're talking high-end presentation software. Slide-Rocket is a premium PowerPoint alternative that's packed with features.

Import a PowerPoint presentation or start from scratch with the theme library. Embed images, charts, videos, transitions, special effects—all of which can be stored, searched for later and shared with others. Live data from real-time feeds online can also be embedded (slides automatically update with the latest information).

Extra capabilities include version control and privacy control—decide who can view, edit or share your slides—plus metrics to track who is viewing your slideshow, where they viewed it, who they've shared it with, and which slides they looked at and for how long. SlideRocket presentations are also HTML5 compatible.

Zoho Show

Zoho Show's presentation software is a cloud-based option that supports the import of many file types (.ppt, .pptx, .pps, .ppsx, .odp, .sxi) and retains the look of the original document when viewed online. As a PowerPoint alternative, Zoho's clean and simple interface is easy to navigate.

Anyone creating business presentations will appreciate the custom flowcharts and diagrams, complete with dynamic shapes and connectors. Enhance your presentations with pictures and videos embedded straight from the web, Picasa and Flickr, and add effects or touch-ups in seconds using the image editor. To make things more interesting, there's a wide gallery of animation and slide transition effects, too. Plus, Zoho enables universal style changes in a snap through the master slide feature, which rolls out changes to every slide thereafter. Version tracking is supported, as is real-time collaboration with other users. You can choose who has permission to edit or view your presentation.

Ready to show off your final product? Send a link to your business presentation, publish it to Zoho's Public Presentations section or embed it on your website.

SlideSnack

SlideSnack is a relatively new and basic option for making slideshows and slidecasts (presentation + voice).

Start by uploading your documents (PowerPoint, Keynote, Word) as PDFs, then design a slideshow from the available templates. You can also record comments for a voice-over. Slidecasts can then be downloaded as video and uploaded to YouTube, Vimeo or any other video-sharing service. As for sharing, your presentations can be embedded on your blog or website for all the world to see.

Microphones & Tech Toys

Microphones are usually counterproductive for small groups. They cause the speaker to talk in an amplified monotone, which can put the audience to sleep. You're better off using your own vocal power, if you can make yourself heard at the back of the room. Without a microphone, you'll try harder, you'll have better inflection and the audience will listen more carefully.

Some points to remember when using tech toys to support your presentation:

- If your room requires amplification for you to be heard, have the sound system adjusted so that you can speak with as much of your own volume as possible.

- The high-intensity projector is the most common tool. It can be directly connected to your laptop or iPad to display your slides or images. This has several advantages once you get to know the software program you have chosen, but be sure to practice using it. Many speakers think they can use a software program after only ten to twenty minutes of preparation. But if you want to be effective and connect with the audience, learn to use the program properly. Use it for both rehearsal and design. The biggest advantage is ease of use, which saves you time.

- If you are using a projector with any regularity, remember Murphy's law and expect trouble. Sooner or later, a bulb will go out, a computer will shut down or a projector will lose its power. If it's an important presentation, bring two of everything.

- If you don't have to turn the house lights down all the way, don't. Keep the room lit as much as possible so that you can see your audience and they can see you. Darkened rooms are an invitation to drowsiness—especially after lunch.

- Once you have created a presentation, it can be easily adapted for different audiences. The range of effects can be quite dazzling. Be careful not to overdo it, as this can distract your audience from your message. Take a class in the use of your program. The presentation software program and the projector do not replace your skill or make up for any shortcomings in your presentation. In fact, they will showcase you, good or bad.

- Don't compete. If you are going to use a professionally produced audiovisual piece in your presentation for a change of pace, make sure it's no longer than seven minutes. Audiences perceive video clips as more authoritative or somehow better than slides with sound. But when asked to guess the length of business films or tapes, the average person guesses double the actual viewing time. Often, the best option is to close with a video, since they are usually so good that you cannot compete.

- Using these tools will give the audience the impression that you are up to date with technology, and they will expect you to deliver on that promise. However, you are the most important audiovisual, the most visible part of the presentation, and that is what the audience came to hear and see. Tools alone will not impress the audience; they have already sat through too many boring, over-produced, computer-generated presentations.

Killer Presentation Tech Tools

Your conference room may be outfitted for top-notch presentations, but how about your briefcase? These days, neither potential customers nor investors have the patience for subpar slideshows.

Here are four tools that will help you make stellar presentations anywhere you go:

1. **Epson PowerLite 1761W WXGA 3LCD projector:**
Make cinema-worthy presentations with this portable 3.7-pound LCD projector, which boasts 2,600 lumens of brightness and 720p resolution, comparable to that of a high-definition television. The short-throw projector sits right next to a screen, making it ideal for a variety of rooms. You can present wirelessly from a laptop, iPhone, iPad, or Android device over a Wi-Fi network using Epson's iProjection app.

2. **Jabra Solemate speaker:**
If your slide show includes sound, laptop speakers won't do. Turn up the volume with this rugged portable speaker, which connects wirelessly with any Bluetooth device, including laptops, tablets, and smartphones. The brick-sized 1.3-pound Solemate, which comes in black or white, has three front speakers and an integrated subwoofer for deep bass. The battery lasts eight hours fully charged.

3. **SlideShark app:**

This app lets you view and present PowerPoint slide shows using your iPad, iPhone or iPod Touch, without compromising animations and graphics. You can store presentations in an online SlideShark account and connect your tablet or smartphone to a projector to display presentations. You can also beam slide shows to mobile devices in the audience and track views.

4. **Targus Ultralife wireless mouse and presenter:**

Use this two-in-one device as a wireless mouse for controlling a cursor. Then, twist the top portion to reveal presentation controls, including buttons for paging up and down and switching to a blank screen. The 5.4-ounce Ultralife, which works with PCs and Macs, has a 1,200-dots-per-inch laser sensor for precise cursor control and works from up to thirty feet away in presentation mode.

On-Camera Techniques

If your presentation is being recorded before a live audience, ignore the camera and focus on the audience. Likewise, if you're being interviewed before a camera, remember that the viewer expects to see you communicating with your live audience or the interviewer, not the camera.

When you go to a TV studio to be interviewed on television and they offer you makeup, accept it. The purpose of the makeup is to eliminate glare and give you a more natural look.

If you perspire under strong TV lights, wipe any obvious perspiration off immediately before you go on the air and again during breaks. Keep tissues in your pocket or very close by. Sweat beading on your forehead or on your lip will make you appear apprehensive, frightened and insincere. If it is a serious problem, get a can of aerosol antiperspirant, spray it on a tissue and dab it on the areas where you sweat most.

If a television reporter is interviewing you, keep your comments short and to the point. TV stations have a habit of editing, sometimes to the point of distorting your statements. Remember, if you're a "good news" story, your comments will be edited to reflect that: local entrepreneur does well. If there is controversy, well, that's great for ratings and the piece will be edited to highlight the conflict: if it bleeds, it leads. Your best way to ensure the message you want to convey gets to your audience is to keep it brief, clear and simple.

If you face a hostile interview on camera, avoid looking surprised. Don't pretend that you don't know why you are there. The only preparation is to expect questions like this and not let them lead you into unwarranted confessions, admissions or explanations. Don't act guilty; otherwise, the audience will assume you are guilty even if you are not.

A Road Warrior's Experience

When I went to Australia on a speaking tour early in my career, I made a classic assumption regarding equipment and logistics. I had been spoiled, accustomed to working with a very professional and tech-savvy team at Redken USA, and I assumed that everyone knew about this stuff! Australia had a very different system for audiovisuals, different electrical voltage and different computer programs. Fortunately for me, the sponsors were resourceful and used to North

Americans and their assumptions.

On my return, I related my experience to a friend, who was a pilot, and he suggested I develop a checklist so that I would never again experience that degree of anxiety and chaos before a presentation. I decided that if this approach worked for a professional pilot, it would probably also help me.

The following checklist will help ensure the success of your presentations. It is extremely helpful to go through this list several days beforehand. After completing several presentations, you will have a good idea of what you require. At that point, you can customize your list. Good preparation will decrease the amount of stress involved, and allow you to have more energy to be yourself.

Consider sending part of this list ahead of time to the meeting planner at the facility where you are making your presentation. Leave one checklist with the equipment, and send one ahead to the event sponsor or organizer, noting what you will bring and what they are required to provide. Keep one list with you so that you can check things off upon your arrival. I advise you to keep it on your person, together with copies of any computer-generated presentations, just in case your briefcase or suitcase gets lost!

Be prepared to succeed, or be prepared for stress.

Presentation Checklist

Projector
_____ Spare bulb
_____ Compatibility with your device
_____ Check bulb
_____ Focused and set to fill screen
_____ Sound level check

Facilities

_____ Whom to call for help and the phone number (work, cell)

_____ Restroom location

_____ Phone location

_____ Snack location

_____ Stairs/elevator location

_____ Fire alarm procedures

_____ Signs for directions to meeting

_____ Parking facilities/accommodation

_____ Location of photocopier

_____ Phone number for messages

Room

_____ Check light controls and set levels

_____ Temperature controls

_____ Disconnect phone in room

_____ Chairs/table arrangement

_____ Extension cord

_____ Tape down electrical cords

_____ Coat rack

_____ Lectern

_____ Water pitcher and glasses

_____ Location of electrical outlets

_____ Position of spotlights

Flip Chart

_____ Paper supply

_____ Markers

_____ Check ink in markers

Music

_____ Cued

_____ Sound level check

Screen

_____ Location

_____ Size

DVD and Automated A/V

_____ Check controls

_____ Cued

_____ Sound level set

_____ Arrive an hour early

_____ Technician on standby

_____ Backup or bypass alternatives

Microphones

_____ Wireless attachment

_____ Sound check

_____ Backup mic

Whiteboard

_____ Dry-erasable pens

_____ Eraser

_____ Clean board

Refreshments

_____ Coffee

_____ Tea

_____ Decaffeinated coffee/tea

_____ Juice

_____ Soft drinks

_____ Water/other

Final Mini-Rehearsal

_____ Opening

_____ Sequence check

_____ Conclusion

Audience Supplies

_____ Notepads

_____ Pencils

_____ Handouts

_____ Place cards

_____ Badges

_____ Roster for presenter/participants

_____ Agenda

_____ Table for supplies

CHAPTER 5

◎ The Target

This chapter is meant to improve your vision, effectively bringing the target closer and making it easier to hit the bull's eye. This I know to be true:

The more I focus on me, the greater my anxiety.

The more I focus on the audience, the lower my anxiety.

The target represents the audience, which is the most important element of any presentation. Audience members preselect the type of event that they wish to attend, whether for business, education or some other purpose. As a presenter, you need to know as much as possible about your audience.

I have witnessed both failures and tremendous successes by all kinds of speakers. But failure comes most often when the speaker forgets about the audience. Many professionals are polished, almost to perfection, almost machine-like, having memorized, studied and perfected every move, but the audience does not want perfection; they want real, authentic people sharing knowledge and experience. Audiences are demanding of all speakers and performers, and the best advice I can give you is be yourself—authentic—and be careful not to fall into the trap of trying to emulate a speaker you admire. The exposure, experience and knowledge of today's audience are as wide as they are deep, and the audience will know when you copy, emulate or tell someone else's story. As Katharine Hepburn said, "You learn in life that the only person you can really correct and change is yourself."

The modern audience will forgive hesitation, nervousness and technical glitches, but they will never forgive disrespect or arrogance on the part of the speaker. Showing off, winging it, and pretending familiarity or a depth of knowledge you don't possess all show disrespect for your audience. They also indicate a great deal of arrogance on the part of the speaker if he or she believes that, in this day of sophistication, the audience can be so easily duped.

The audience expects and demands more, having seen in person or watched on video some of the world's best speakers. Although they do not expect you to match that level of performance, they do expect you to bring the one thing all of these speakers have in common—authenticity and very good presenting skills. Today's audience has "been there, done that" and has a high degree of cynicism, which can only be overcome with sincerity and competence. Remember, they can and will tweet about you as you speak, research a point you make and record your performance, posting it on YouTube using their smartphones while you are onstage. The days of "fake it till you make it" are long gone!

The audience wants you to answer three questions:

1. What is your company's product or service? With the proliferation of brands and divisions, it is hard to tell who does what or when or where.

2. What does your company stand for? Today, the audience wants to know all the details. With their superior awareness and access to information, they know that one division may be working for the environment, whereas another division of the same company may be charged with environmental damage.

3. What kind of reputation does your company have? Are you prepared to live up to your company's reputation? Are you who you say you are? The audience wants to know the truth and will eventually find it. Trust is the number one issue for today's audience.

This chapter has two sections.

The first section focuses on you, the speaker, and how you interact with the audience.

And the second section deals with the audience and what you need to know about them to be a powerful speaker.

You & the Audience

The Audience's Attention

Keep it and cherish it! Be realistic about your audience's attention span. Most North Americans have been trained to focus for short bursts of time. By the time we reach high school, we have been trained by watching twenty-four hours of television per week. And it doesn't stop there. The number of hours per year the average American youth watches television is 1,200, compared with 900 hours spent in school. Here's another statistic: 67 percent of Americans regularly watch television while eating dinner.

By the time we reach college or university, we have been thoroughly trained to dole out short measures of attention—we didn't sign up for that; it happened unconsciously. During commercial breaks we go to the washroom, get snacks or drinks, shift the cushions, read our iPads and return phone calls. Yes, we have been trained.

An average hour of monitored prime-time U.S. network TV programming contains seven minutes and fifty-nine seconds of in-show brand appearances and thirteen minutes and fifty-two seconds of network commercial messages, for a combined total of twenty-one minutes and fifty-one seconds of marketing content, according to TNS Media Intelligence. These commercial messages account for 36 percent of an average prime-time hour. And unscripted reality programming has an average of thirteen minutes and fifty-two seconds per hour of brand appearances, compared with just five minutes and fifty-six seconds per hour for scripted programs such as sitcoms and dramas, reported TNS. What this means for presenters, speakers and facilitators is that every twelve to fourteen minutes, we need to change pace or tempo, use a visual aid, move on the stage or otherwise shift the audience's attention.

To keep your audience's attention, cover only the essential points. Ask yourself what information is necessary for your audience to have at this time (remembering the 10 percent rule). Always present your main or strongest point first. Include the benefits and reasons why the audience should accept the ideas, plans or products presented. Remember, the audience is always thinking, "What's in it for me?" or WI-FM. When writing your presentation, put yourself in the audience's shoes and list some of the possible benefits for them if they were to take action based on your point of view. However, make sure that the benefits are real and tangible, based on the true outcome of your point of view. Potential benefits might include an improvement or increase in one or more of the following: availability, efficiency, performance, uniqueness, reliability, convenience, maintenance, cost, profit, safety, status, beauty, comfort, size, quality, utility, strength, schedule, goodwill, service, compactness, lightness, quantity, weight and speed. Use evidence to substantiate any claims that you make.

Some techniques for keeping your audience's attention:

Speak Up
Talk a little louder than you think you have to. Most people speak far too softly and it sounds like they are mumbling. Speaking up also helps calm your anxiety or nervousness.

Use Gestures
Use your hands and body language to punctuate what you say and convey energy and enthusiasm.

Use Illustrations

The listener's mind is hungry for images. Describe your idea clearly so that they can envision it. Give them something to see. Use analogies and stories so that they can visualize along with you.

Personalize It

Use first-person stories whenever possible. The audience perks up when they hear phrases like "The other day I..." or "I have found from my own experience..." and "A friend of mine once told me..."

Pause Occasionally

Pauses might be the most effective technique for regaining the attention of an audience. Most speakers do not use this powerful technique because the silence seems deafening to them. However, the audience welcomes the pause. They usually relax and refocus. Try it and you will see all eyes looking back at you, waiting for your next statement.

Reserve Handouts

Save handouts until after your presentation or for during a break. If you give people handouts at the beginning of your talk, they will read them instead of paying attention to you, so save them for pickup as they leave.

Use Rhetorical Questions

Using rhetorical questions such as "What would you think if...?" forces people to respond mentally, hence keeping them on track with you.

Use Reinforcing Questions

When you ask questions such as "What have you learned so far?" or "Where can you apply this?" or "Does this make sense?" the listener will then assess and engage with the content of your presentation.

Your Listening Habits

Your listening habits affect how you speak. No one is born with the ability to listen effectively. Just like all other communication skills, good listening must be learned. To a great extent, this involves breaking old habits and forming new ones.

Here is a short test, which, if answered honestly, will give you an idea of whether you could improve your listening habits. It will also give you a better understanding of your audience, because you will need to put yourself in their place. Yes, I know there are exceptions, so base your answer on what you do the most.

Please answer yes or no:

Y / N   You think about four times faster than a person usually talks. Do you use this excess time to think about other things while you're keeping track of the conversation?

Y / N   Do you listen primarily for facts rather than ideas when someone is speaking?

Y / N   Do you avoid listening to things you feel will be too difficult to understand?

Y / N   Can you tell from a person's appearance and delivery whether they will have anything worthwhile to say?

Y / N   When somebody is talking to you, do you try to make him/her think you're paying attention when you're not?

Y / N   Do certain words or phrases prejudice you so that you cannot listen objectively?

Y / N   Do you turn your thoughts to other subjects when you believe a speaker will have nothing particularly interesting to say?

Y / N   When you're listening to someone, are you easily distracted by outside sights and sounds?

Y / N   When you are puzzled or annoyed by what someone says, do you try to get the question straightened out immediately, either in your own mind or by interrupting the speaker?

Y / N   In a conversation, do you catch yourself concentrating more on what you are going to say when it's your turn to speak than on what the speaker is saying?

If you truthfully answered "no" to all the questions, you are a rare individual—perhaps a perfect listener. (You may also be kidding yourself!) Every "yes" means you have a habit that impairs your ability to listen and communicate effectively—and therefore to successfully communicate at the front of the room.

The Halo Effect

The audience typically perceives you differently from how you judge yourself. I call this the Halo Effect. Essentially, most people dislike or fear public speaking, so when someone else gets up to speak, the listener is in a state of admiration, and even gratitude, because it is not them speaking (this is very often true in office or business presentations). Many in the audience don't particularly care about your speaking style; they want to know, learn and be inspired to do what you do.

Our informal surveys (done before the Presentation Power workshops over a period of five years) show that within any audience are the following emotions:

Admiration (30 percent)
Interest (30 percent)
Distraction (30 percent)
Criticism (10 percent)

The Halo Effect

Thirty percent admire you just because you are speaking. They are relieved that it is you, instead of them, speaking at the front of the room.

Thirty percent listen because they are interested in the subject, and they also admire you because you are speaking.

Thirty percent are distracted or they have an internal agenda, so they are not fully available to listen or interact.

Ten percent listen with discernment and judgment.

In audience surveys, most listeners give the presenter about three to five minutes to warm up. After that, their more critical judgment will surface. There is one thing all audiences seem to hate—apathy on the part of the presenter. Demonstrate that you care, and they will, too; if you don't, they won't either.

The Swan Effect

What the audience doesn't see is how fast your heart is beating or the sweaty palms or the number of hours you spent preparing and rehearsing so that you could deliver this speech.

In my workshop, I use the analogy of the swan on the lake: the swan looks like it is gently gliding upon the surface of the water, beautiful, serene and effortless. All the while, inside the swan, its heart is beating rapidly and its feet beneath the surface are paddling hard. It takes more effort and energy for the swan to get airborne than it does to actual fly. Once the swan is flying, it can ride the wind, use updrafts—

well, so can you once you get started.

Remember, you are not transparent. They will not see your heart beating hard. Nor do they know where or when you speech is supposed to end or exactly what you are supposed to say. So relax, fire up and speak up. Give your voice flight.

The Swan Effect

The Audience & You

Audience Analysis

Who is my audience? Every audience starts with an agenda— remember, they are always consciously or unconsciously asking them themselves "What's in it for me?" The more accurately you can define the demographics, the more ac-curately you can define the needs and write your script to satisfy both your and the audience's agenda.

There are three kinds of speakers:

1. Ego-centric speakers give the talk they want to give. They have something to say and don't care about the audience, except to get them to hear what they have to say.

2. Other-centric speakers deliver a talk that the audience wants to hear, often using words, concepts, stories and visuals that resonate with audience members, in the hope that this connection will allow the speaker to lead or influence the audience.

3. Topic-centric speakers deliver a talk about a specific topic and share their knowledge, which is often the only reason the audience is present or willing to listen.

But how do you know what the audience wants to hear? How do you know what will resonate with them? How do you know what they are thinking?

The answer is audience analysis, the process of learning who your audience is, what they are thinking and how you can best reach them. Thoughtful audience analysis will help you understand your audience's perspective and provide you with the insights you need to persuade, challenge or inform them. Thorough audience analysis will provide information that will help you focus your message. By selecting the most effective content and visuals, you can tailor your delivery to hit the target audience how and where you want.

Audience analysis contains three primary dimensions:

1. **Demographic Analysis:**

   Who is in your audience? What are their individual and group characteristics?

2. **Psychological Analysis:**

   What does your audience know? What do they believe? What do they think about your topic?

3. **Contextual Analysis:**

   When and where are you presenting? Why is this audience listening to you?

Always remember that you are speaking to individuals. In rare circumstances, you may be able to meet privately with some of the audience members before your presentation to learn about them and their expectations. I often ask the organizer to circulate a short questionnaire to a small sample of my audience in advance, but this isn't always possible. Usually, you will need to infer a great deal from your audience analysis instead.

You don't talk to unknown, faceless people known as audiences. You talk to individual people, and no two people in your audience are identical. Although the individuals in your audience may be similar in many ways, there will always be a range of knowledge levels, beliefs and expectations. Even the best audience analysis will have a degree of inaccuracy and guesswork buried within it.

Find a quiet space and analyze the audience on your own, be curious and imagine you're in the audience. Put yourself in the front row—would you listen? Ask yourself "Who will attend?" You might even ask yourself "Will I like them?"

The following questions are designed to help you focus on the audience, determine who they are and listen to them more clearly:

Who is your audience—age, gender, sexual orientation, education, profession?

Why is the audience here—are they pro or con your topic?

What is their relationship to you?

What are their expectations?

What are your assumptions?

Does the topic/story fit the audience?

What do they want to learn?

How much do they know already?

What do you want them to know—background, immediate situation and future?

What will make it easy for the audience to understand?

Do you need visuals and/or written support, endorsements, research papers or studies?

How to get the answers to the questions about your audience:

Interview the event organizer

Interview audience members

Survey your audience members

Research industry trends

Poll people similar to your audience

Study past event archives

Review current event materials

Make observations at the event itself

Audience Trends

> "You get people to do what you want not by bullying them or tricking them, but by understanding them."
> — Anonymous

Today's audience is composed of independent thinkers who seek control over their lives. This group has witnessed the revelations of Bradley Manning and WikiLeaks founder Julian Assange, and Edward Snowden's massive CIA leak. They have seen one of the largest stock market crashes, the fall and rise of Apple under Steve Jobs, the fall of Microsoft, the Iraq War and the War in Afghanistan. They understood global warming long before politicians. They have seen senators resigning their positions in the face of public scrutiny. This audience has become very skeptical about trusting elected officials and has a high degree of cynicism as a result. They are educated and sophisticated, with more post-secondary education than any other generation before them. Most have had two distinct careers, or two functions within the same career. They know how to find out what is going on and how to access information that was once reserved for a select few. They ask questions and expect to get the answers.

They seek a higher quality of life. They have had bigger and more, and now they want better quality and less stress in the process, and they are willing to pay for it. They are interested in spiritual growth and its application to their day-to-day lives.

They are extremely demanding and becoming less tolerant of poor service. This audience is aware of consumer power and how to use it. With consumer advocacy on the rise, and various media outlets reporting on individuals who have been "cheated," this trend will only grow. They will no longer just sit and take it, not from anyone. They won't get mad; they'll just let you and everyone else know about it.

They are optimistic but well grounded in reality; they have had boom times and hard times and will work to create the best for themselves. They will support businesses and governments that help them. They want to be self-supporting, while retaining their independence and lifestyle.

They are increasingly proactive in environmentalism, and this will become a more powerful motivator in the future and influence their choices dramatically.

Often, organizations and individuals hold on to what they know, creating problems for themselves because of their inflexibility towards change in a world where change can happen overnight and be reported and analyzed the next day.

This audience is far less politically homogeneous. At one time in North America, you could have described the political parties as Republican and Democrat in the U.S., and NDP, Conservative and Liberal in Canada, and had a fairly good idea of what these different parties represented. Today, we have the right wing or left wing of all parties and tremendous overlap on issues and conflict about what they represent. Now, rather than being loyal to any one party, people are motivated more by the specific issues and values that they deem important.

Financial & Technical Presentations

Tell it like it is. Gear your talk to the audience's level of sophistication, regardless of the level of expertise. You'll do well to eliminate or de-emphasize jargon. The greater level of technical sophistication of your listeners, the more important is the use of analogy. If you listen to mathematicians talking to each other, they use folk expressions and simple English. They're trying to convey broad concepts within a narrow, nonverbal language. Remember, even though the subject matter is technical, you're still talking to human beings. People will get bored, daydream and react irritably even during a serious presentation. Keep your talk upbeat, fast-paced and simple.

And keep visuals simple and save your details for handouts. Include all references and sources of information. Accept the fact that technical talks are not the same as technical papers. You can speak at a maximum rate of 160 words per minute; therefore, it's impossible to dwell upon detail. Just hit the key points, focus on the concepts and give the backup material as a handout.

They say in the financial field, stay focused on the bottom line. Use bottom-line psychology when delivering financial reports. Tell the audience the result, the bottom-line number, immediately, and then tell them how you got there. If you try to save the answers until your explanation, many impatient questions and queries will interrupt you.

Speaking to Young People

Business presenters are occasionally asked to speak to a young audience. This could be day campers, youth associations or school groups of all ages. Never turn down a chance to speak to youth. These occasions are often the most potent learning experiences for public speakers. Children detect and reject insincerity instantly. This is true from preschool age right through to early adulthood. Speaking to young listeners will help you communicate naturally and directly.

The younger the audience, the more important it is to speak at eye level. If you're communicating with a four- or five-year-old, sit down in a chair or even on the floor. With children, there's virtually no communication without direct eye contact or visual reinforcement.

Confucius said, "The ultimate evil is the ability to make abstract that which is concrete." The moral of this is that children like straight talk about real things and real objects. They like people with names and faces. They get impatient with generalizations.

Don't talk down to young people. Condescension is another form of phoniness and kids don't like it. If you want to get a message across, tell them a story with subtle moral lessons. Kids buy facts but not philosophy.

If you want to communicate effectively with teenagers, get them involved during your talk. Make it a freewheeling conversation, Socratic in style. Teenagers have great energy and imagination. Go for direction rather than control when speaking to a room full of teens.

Adults are kids at heart. The lessons you learn from speaking to young listeners are directly applicable to your communication with an adult audience, even in a business environment. Be open, honest and sincere. Keep your eyes on your listeners' eyes. Avoid abstractions. Get your listeners involved in what you are talking about.

Conclusion

You Have a Choice

Here is one more tool to help you become a powerful speaker. After every presentation, ask yourself the following three questions:

1. **What worked?**
    Identify what you did well, what the audience liked. It is easy to be self-critical and harder to be honestly self-aware.

2. **What did not work?**
    Most people think they know the answer to this question but forget to ask the audience and are often surprised when they get a completely different answer. Remember, the audience's opinion is the most important.

3. **What can I do differently?**
    If you don't ask this, you will not improve, because this question gives you permission and requires you to change and grow.

Becoming a powerful speaker is a life-long journey, and reading this book is your first step. This is just the beginning. Now you are well informed, so your next step is to put your knowledge to use, immediately—now! As you use the knowledge and tools, you will become more powerful and useful to the world; you will show up and make a difference. Use these tools until you no longer notice them. Read this book again within thirty days and watch other speakers through the context of what you have learned. Become the eternal student. Get out there and make mistakes, experiment and try it out. You have a choice: put this book down, never to pick it up again, or become a truly authentic speaker. What will it be?

Having the power to communicate will affect you more than you can imagine. The ability to engage, influence and motivate others is an amazing power. It will help you get what you want, so use it wisely. It will bring opportunities and people to you, and open doors you thought closed. Becoming a powerful speaker starts and finishes with you. Have fun, and always show up!

Recommended Reading

The following books have influenced my work and offer interesting perspectives on the art of great presenting:

Talent is Overrated: What Really Separates World-Class Performers from Everybody Else by Geoff Colvin

On Bullshit by Harry G. Fankfurt

Outliers; The Tipping Point; and *Blink* by Malcolm Gladwell

Linchpin and *The Icarus Deception* by Seth Godin

Emotional Intelligence: Why It Can Matter More Than IQ by Daniel Goleman

Fascinate: Your 7 Triggers to Persuasion and Captivation by Sally Hogshead

Metaphors We Live By by George Lakoff and Mark Johnson

Psycho-Cybernetics: A New Way to Get More Living Out of Life by Maxwell Maltz

Trust Me: Four Steps to Authenticity and Charisma by Nick Morgan

Drive and *A Whole New Mind* by Daniel Pink

Selling Sucks: How to Stop Selling and Start Getting Prospects to Buy! by Frank J. Rumbauskas Jr.

The Story Factor: Inspiration, Influence, and Persuasion through the Art of Storytelling by Annette Simmons

World Famous: How to Give Your Business a Kick-Ass Brand Identity by David Tyreman

About the Author

Geoffrey X. Lane is an internationally acclaimed public speaker, presentation director and consultant. He has been coaching executives, public speakers and other professionals in communications, media relations and presentation techniques for more than twenty-five years. Known as the "Million Dollar Coach," Geoffrey has helped business leaders secure millions of dollars in contracts, including the successful Vancouver 2010 Olympic bid. Now President and CEO of Lane Consulting Group, he has lectured at the University of British Columbia's Sauder School of Business and Faculty of Commerce.

In his presentations, workshops and seminars, Geoffrey offers proven techniques for delivering presentations with clarity, authenticity and power. His audiences walk away with enhanced confidence and self-awareness. They also take with them valuable tools to present information and sell ideas effectively, giving them a powerful edge over competitors.

INDEX

Page numbers in *italics* refer to figures

3M flip charts, 94, 97
10 percent rule, *64*, 64–65, 117
2010 Winter Olympics. *See*
   Vancouver Winter Olympic bid
   team

A
adrenaline, 29–31, 43
alcohol, 34, 43
alliteration, 47
Altman, Robert, 9
amplification. *See* microphones;
   sound system; speakers (sound);
   volume
analogies, 47. *See also* storytelling
animation, 94, 99, 100, 101, 105
anxiety. *See* fear and anxiety
appearance, 51–53, 96, 119. *See also*
   body language; facial expressions; gestures; makeup
Apple, 78–79, 89, 128
apps, 104, 105
archer, 15, 16, *16*, 21–55. *See also*
   appearance; archer model;
   authenticity; body language;
   charisma; clothing; energy, of
   presenter; facial expressions;
   fear and anxiety; focus, of
   presenter; gestures; passion;
   performance level; preparation;
   rehearsal; relaxation; visualization; voice
archer model, *15*, 15–18. *See also*
   archer; arrow; bow; target

Armstrong, Peter, 79
arrow, 15, 16, 17, *17*, 21, 57–85.
   See also archer model; audience; humor; introductions;
   metaphors; opening remarks;
   question and answer period;
   presentation don'ts, scripts;
   story arc; storytelling; team
   presentations
Assange, Julian, 128
audience
analysis or research of, 51, 52, 55, 63,
   113, 119, 123–127
attention span, 75, 116–119
and authenticity of presenter,
   36–42, 52, 85, 114
and clothing of presenter, 51–53, 96
eye contact with, 68, 75, 131
feedback from, 133
and financial presentations, 130
and gestures, 46–48, 117
hecklers, 85
and humor, 48, 70–71
and introductions, 67, 71–72, 73
and lighting, 98, 103
motivations and needs of, 18, 22,
   43, 57–58, 65, 66, 115, 117, 129
and opening remarks, 67–68, 122
perceptions of speaker, 106,
   121–123
and presentation tools, 17, 87,
   89–92, 94, 95, 98, 99, 103–104,
   105
questions from, 70, 74–76, 85

Learn more about Geoffrey X. Lane on his website:
www.geoffreyxlane.com

For information about Geoffrey's Presentation Power ™
Workshops, visit: **www.presentationpower.com**

Discover more "Hidden Secrets" to great public speaking!

Presentation Power Podcast
The Million Dollar Coach, Geoffrey X. Lane, presents a special offer: to
receive the "101 Speaking Tips from the Presentation Power Workshop,"
go to www.presentationpower.com and sign up for Geoffrey's podcast.

Keynote Speeches
Geoffrey is also available for keynote speeches on the theme: Influence
+ Impact = Income. This keynote is enlightening and entertaining, and
puts the focus on leadership and authentic communication. Whether you
are a leader, aspire to be a leader, or even if you do not think you are a
leader, you have to demonstrate personal leadership. This keynote offers
insightful and powerful lessons on what you need to do to have greater
results in your work and your life.

Become a "Presentation Director"
If you are a business development or marketing director in the Architect/
Engineer/Construction industry and would like to learn how to how to
become a "Presentation Director" or to teach the concepts and strategies
and lead the "Presentation Power" workshop, please email your résumé
to: gxl@presentationpower.com .

Buy the Presentation Power Ebook
Presentation Power is also available in ebook format. Search for it on
ebook retail sites such as Amazon.com and Kobobooks.com.

*"Nothing happens until communication begins. Great ideas
have no impact until they are given voice, your voice."*
—Geoffrey X. Lane

CPSIA information can be obtained at www.ICGtesting.com
Printed in the USA
LVOW13s0437210314

378279LV00002B/8/P